IN TIMES OF WAR

Messages of wisdom from soldiers in the afterlife

Edited by

JONATHAN BEECHER

A WHITE CROW ANTHOLOGY

www.whitecrowbooks.com

In Times of War

Copyright © 2019 by Jonathan Beecher. All rights reserved.

Published and printed in the United States of America
and the United Kingdom by White Crow Books; an
imprint of White Crow Productions Ltd.

The right of Jonathan Beecher to be identified as the author
of this work has been asserted by him in accordance
with the Copyright, Design and Patents act 1988.

No part of this book may be reproduced, copied or used in any
form or manner whatsoever without written permission, except
in the case of brief quotations in reviews and critical articles.

For information, contact White Crow Books
@ info@whitecrowbooks.com.

Cover Design by Astrid@Astridpaints.com
Interior design by Velin@Perseus-Design.com

Paperback ISBN 978-1-78677-083-7
eBook   ISBN 978-1-78677-084-4

Non-Fiction / Body, Mind & Spirit / Parapsychology / Death & Dying

www.whitecrowbooks.com

Disclaimer: White Crow Productions Ltd. and its directors,
employees, distributors, retailers, wholesalers and assignees disclaim
any liability or responsibility for the author's statements, words,
ideas, criticisms or observations. White Crow Productions Ltd.
assumes no responsibility for errors, inaccuracies, or omissions.

IN TIMES OF WAR

Messages of wisdom from soldiers in the afterlife

The Spring blew trumpets of color;
Her Green sang in my brain—
I saw a blind man groping
'Tap-tap' with his cane;

I pitied him his blindness;
But can I boast *I see?*
Perhaps there walks a spirit
Close by, who pities me,—

A spirit who hears me tapping
The five-sensed cane of the mind,
Amid such unknown glories—
I may be worse than blind.

"Blind" ~ Harry Kemp

CONTENTS

PREFACE ix
INTRODUCTION 1
1. PRIVATE DOWDING 7
2. DEATH ON THE BATTLEFIELD 21
3. NOT QUITE DEAD YET 41
4. PRESIDENT ROOSEVELT'S SECRETARY COMMUNICATES FROM THE AFTERLIFE 65
5. RESCUE CIRCLES 75
6. A CONSCIOUS DISSOLUTION 87
7. ABOVE THE BATTLEFIELDS 97
8. A SOUL IN PURGATORY 103
9. SELFISHNESS 113
10. ONE DAY AS A THOUSAND YEARS 127
CONCLUSION 133
REFERENCES 143

*The world is not my home
I'm just a-passing through*

~ Tom Waits

PREFACE

After weeks of news programs, articles and documentaries leading up to the hundredth anniversary of the end of World War I, I was reminded of an interview some years ago with the second to last surviving combat soldier of that war; an Englishman named Harry Patch,[1] who died in 2009 aged 111.

At the time of his hundredth birthday Harry was thrust into the public spotlight and interviewed about his wartime experiences. When asked about how he subsequently coped with the horrors of war, he recalled an incident on the battlefield:

> We came across this lad from 'A' Company. He was ripped open from his shoulder to his waist by shrapnel, and lying in a pool of blood.

When we got to him he looked at us and said: 'shoot me.'

He was beyond all human help, and before we could draw a revolver he was dead. And the final word he uttered was 'Mother.'

I was with him in the last seconds of his life. It wasn't a cry of despair; it was a cry of surprise and joy.

I think—although I wasn't allowed to see her, I am sure his mother was in the next world to welcome him and he knew it" (van Emden, Patch 2007).

That incident seemed to convince Harry that death is not the end, and I agree with his conclusion, which brings us to the subject of this book.

If you believe, as I used to, that nothing happens after death, I ask you to suspend your disbelief for a while and keep reading. If you believe that something does happen ... I ask that you do the same.

In the autumn of 2000, after suffering a head trauma from falling on my face while walking in my sleep, I found myself feeling as if I had been plugged into a greater reality, which I hesitate to call God because, although I feel there is God, and I am part of it, I don't *know* what God is. What I do know is that prior to knocking myself out I was an ardent atheist and materialist. I wasn't anti-religion and I respected other people's views, I just didn't believe any of it and talk of life after death, psychic phenomena and mediumship, to me, was just psychobabble.

When it came to the subject of death, I was a firm believer that when you're dead you're dead and that's it. I found that worldview quite convenient; no higher

PREFACE

authority to worry about, and the knowledge that one day I would go to sleep and not wake up didn't unduly concern me, although I have to say, death is something I didn't dwell on back then.

After the accident that all changed. When my wife, Victoria, heard a bang in the night and found me lying unconscious on the floor, apparently I looked a mess. One of my front teeth was bashed in, my lip was severed from my face where I'd bitten it, needing thirty stitches, and my jaw was broken on both sides.

"You're in trouble, Jon," I heard her say, and I wondered if I was dreaming. I opened my eyes and saw she was kneeling over me looking distressed. Looking up at her I felt calm and rested ... I had no idea what had just happened and I was not in any pain.

We had some friends staying that night. One, hearing the noise, rushed into the bedroom and demanded that Victoria call an ambulance. Another came in a minute later, took one look at me, rushed to the bathroom and vomited. It was then that I realized maybe I *was* in trouble.

After two days in hospital followed by six weeks of little or no talking and drinking liquidized food through a straw, I healed up and felt physically fine. No big deal, I thought. But something had changed ... I just didn't understand what.

Due to the nature of the break, the doctors decided they wouldn't fix my jaw with a plate because they were concerned that I might be left with palsy. Instead, they wired my mouth almost shut and suggested I take five weeks off work and avoid talking so as to allow my jaw to heal. Although staying at home was not my idea of fun, I took their advice and spent the next month trying to quiet myself.

I started to write a journal, something that had never occurred to me before, and this turned out to be invaluable because I had plenty of time to write down how I was feeling. During the next five years I wrote hundreds of thousands of words.

Strangely, post-accident, I felt I had a "knowing" that there is no death other than the death of the body and my fear of death, if I ever had one, had disappeared. I also had a strong feeling that this isn't home. I remember trying to explain that to a friend shortly afterwards.

"What do you mean this isn't home?" he asked. "You mean this country?"

"No, " I replied, "I mean this planet."

He pulled a face. "So you think you're a f—— alien?"

I shrugged my shoulders. "I know how it sounds," I said. "It sounds mad. I can't explain it and, no, I don't mean I'm an alien. I can't explain it in words. Also, the colors of the trees and plants look brighter," I added, "more lush and, well, ... just different."

"You sound like a girl," he replied, and walked away shaking his head.

One of the earliest changes in my behavior had to do with hunting. I used to shoot game—pheasants mostly—in the winter during the game season. The accident happened at the end of October and by December I was getting back to normal. A friend of mine called me because we had some shooting days booked in January. I told him straight away, "I can't go shooting—I can't kill an animal."

"What are you talking about?" he replied. "You've been killing them for years."

I didn't understand why, I just knew that I could no longer do it.

A few months later I was in Spain with some friends. We were sitting in a bar and a cockroach ran across the floor. Someone jumped up and stamped on it. My instant reaction was to retch ... I almost vomited.

PREFACE

Vomiting over a cockroach ... that felt weird. Not understanding why I had become so sensitive bothered me but, at the same time, I felt more contented than I'd ever felt before. It was as if there was an old me and a new me and I oscillated between the two. For a while I wondered if I was having a nervous breakdown. Some friends thought I'd found God. "But I wasn't looking for God" I'd say. "I was doing okay on my own."

I arrived at a dinner party one evening and one of the guests came up to me and whispered, "Don't talk about all that afterlife stuff or Paul (the host) won't invite you again." It didn't stop me talking, but it was very disconcerting because I was now thinking completely differently than before the accident and it took a while before I began to realize that these *new feelings* had somehow been caused by that accident.

It was as if I'd had a software update. I didn't go through a tunnel or meet a beautiful being, at least I have no memory of it ... I just banged my head and woke up to a whole new worldview.

What followed was a series of psychic events and synchronicities, which led me along different paths and eventually I started reading the near-death experience and life after death literature. Prior to that I thought a near-death experience was a lucky escape or a close shave—I had no idea about the spiritual transformations that certain people experience after an injury or illness. It was then that I discovered that people all over the world experience what I was going through every day—there are lots of them.

I don't know if I had a near-death experience. I didn't feel as if I was near death but it was certainly a spiritually transformative event that turned out to be life changing.

Today, what I can say without hesitation is, that *I know* the death of the physical body is nothing but a transition to another state or vibration. I don't know how I know this; I just know. But at the same time my logical brain tells me that *I don't know anything*, for what is *knowing* but a feeling? It's truly paradoxical.

Early on in my search for more answers I came across Victor Zammit's book, *A Lawyer Presents the Case for the Afterlife*[2] In it he cited an Australian researcher named Cherie Sutherland who listed the typical effects that a near-death experience (NDE) or a spiritually-transformative experience (STE) has on people's lives. The list included:

1. A universal belief in life after death
2. A high proportion (80%) now believed in reincarnation
3. A total absence of fear of death
4. A large shift from organized religion to personal spiritual practice
5. A statistically significant increase in psychic sensitivity
6. A more positive view of self and of others
7. An increased desire for solitude
8. An increased sense of purpose
9. A lack of interest in material success coupled with a marked increase in interest in spiritual development
10. Fifty per cent experienced major difficulties in close relationships as a result of their changed priorities:
    an increase in health consciousness
    most drank less alcohol
    almost all gave up smoking
    most gave up prescription drugs
    most watched less television
    most read fewer newspapers

PREFACE

11. An increased interest in alternative healing
12. An increased interest in learning and self-development
13. Seventy-five percent experienced a major career change in which they moved towards areas of helping others.

I read that list and realized that I could tick nearly every box and more.

I experienced another event in 2002 when a friend of mine (who I'll call B) who had died in my house fourteen years earlier, seemingly sent a message to me by "dropping in"[3] to a sitting with a medium who happened to be giving a reading to the wife of a friend of my sister (the wife I'll call M).

M's husband then contacted my sister to tell her M had been to see a medium and had a message for me from a friend of mine who had died in my house.

My sister later told me that she wouldn't have even considered asking me to speak to M because she knew I had no belief or interest in anything like that, had it not been for what M told her. M described the "death scene" of my friend with detailed accuracy. On the day B died I was in shock after I found his body and I called my sister and she came over and helped clear up the blood and vomit left on the carpet. Only myself, my girlfriend, my sister, the police, a doctor, and the people who picked up his body saw the death scene and it's highly unlikely that M would have had detailed knowledge of it, fourteen years later. That convinced my sister to call me, and in turn I called M.

It was then that M told me she had a message from my departed friend. At the time I didn't know anything about mediums but a few days prior to that call B had come into my mind, and that prompted me to write in my journal about the night of his death in 1988, something I hadn't done before. While I wrote I questioned whether I could have done anything about his death, such as take him to hospital (he was drunk), and if I had, whether he would still be alive today?

The medium told M that I had been thinking about my friend recently and that there was nothing I could have done about his death because it was his time to go.

The fact that I received a message from someone unknown to me telling me I had been "thinking about my friend recently" and answering a question that I'd written down just a few days before, and giving me information about me and B that she couldn't have known about, intrigued me. He had been dead for fourteen years and I didn't think about him often, but I had been that week and I'd been writing about him.

Of course, I have no idea if my deceased friend really did contact me but I was now open to the possibility, and as a result, a year later I decided that I wanted to experience a sitting with a medium for myself.

I had read some of the skeptical literature because I am by nature a skeptic and before my first visit I learned about cold reading, muscle reading, fishing, (where a person fishes for clues), and I thought about what a medium could possibly know about me before I met them.

My first experience was highly evidential but I don't have the space to detail it here. That led to more sittings. When I sat with a medium I kept my mind open and my mouth mostly shut. If the medium said "does that make sense?" I might say yes or no, but in general, I'd keep quiet until after the session and if I did receive information I'd mentally group it into "known," "unknown" and "false."

Over time, people came through claiming to be my father, stepmother, uncle, grandmother, great aunt,

PREFACE

grandfather, step-grandmother, daughter, two friends, and a former business partner, and they often gave me information, messages and advice, which the medium couldn't possibly have had knowledge of. In some cases I was told things that *I didn't know* until it was verified later.

For instance, one time I was having a Skype conversation with a medium named Isabelle in Belgium. I had asked Isabelle if we could do some Skype sessions where, rather than staying silent during the session, if she said something interesting such as a person's name, I would ask her to focus on that person. It was an experiment. To date we have had six sessions. During two nothing happened; in one I was given detailed information about a deceased person who wanted me to get a message to a living person but I didn't recognize either of the people named. However, two of the sessions were very evidential and on this occasion, while we were chatting, Isabelle mentioned that she was going on a course at the Arthur Findlay College,[4] in England; a college left as a legacy to the Spiritualist movement by the esteemed Scottish psychical researcher, Arthur Findlay, MBE (May 16, 1883 – July 24, 1964).[5] I asked why she was going and she explained that she was having problems "linking," meaning she was getting information psychically but sometimes she couldn't connect the information to the right person.

Then she said, "I have your father's father here."

That was interesting for me because my mother and father separated when I was two years old. My mother remarried soon after and I was given my stepfather's name. I only met my father four times: twice when I was in my late twenties and twice a few days before he died in 2001. I never met my grandparents, nor did I know anything about them. Having grown up with my step-grandparents I'd never really thought about my biological grandparents. At that time there was no way Isabelle could have known that I have a different birth family—most of my friends didn't know that and still don't today.

I asked why he was there and she replied, "He's interested in what you're doing … your work."

I asked her to send him my love and added, "I didn't know my father's parents, I don't even know their names."

We carried on talking and she said, "I've been given the name Edward."

I replied that it's a common name in England but it didn't mean anything to me. A few minutes later she said, "I've been given the name Mary or Maria." Again, I replied saying it didn't mean anything to me and a little while later the conversation ended.

Isabelle didn't seem to know who Edward and Maria were other than they were on my grandparent level (her words). I realize it might sound strange that during the conversation neither of us thought more about who Edward and Mary or Maria might be but Isabelle wasn't fishing for clues, and the last person I expected to hear from was the grandfather whom I had never met or even thought about.

It was only after the session when I played the conversation back and heard myself saying, "I never knew my grandparents, I don't even know their names," that it occurred to me that Edward and Mary or Maria might be my grandparent's names.

I have two brothers from my father's second marriage and after the session I texted one of them and asked, "What were the names of our grandparents?" A few minutes later a text came back; "Edward and Maria." For me, that was good evidence.

PREFACE

I could fill a few chapters here with evidential information that I've received from mediums, and on that occasion, I was particularly impressed that someone could tell me the name of my grandparents when *I* didn't even know their names.

Although Isabelle is a professional medium she has never charged me a cent for her time.

Thus far, I have concluded (rightly or wrongly) from numerous sittings I've had, that the mediums were getting information by using something beyond their five senses and that the communicators might well have been who they said they were.

There are other possibilities. One is that Edward's higher self was communicating, After all, Edward is just the name attributed to that particular body by his parents. Maybe Edward in that sense is no more, and any communication is coming from the part of him that's no longer Edward, such as a higher-self entity that he is a part of.

A priest might say I was communicating with a false spirit (one did tell me that once) or even a devil. A Buddhist might say Edward had reincarnated or that I had been communicating with a hungry ghost; a low-level spirit entity. A parapsychologist might say I was experiencing "super-psi," the idea that the medium was tapping into my mind and everyone else's and retrieving information from some sort of global mind.

An atheist or anyone with a conflicting world-view (as I once had) might say it was a lucky guess or I imagined it or I'd been tricked or I'm lying, but I know that not one of those explanations describe my experiences. There are so many possibilities that we don't have room to contemplate here, but one thing I feel sure about is, my old assumption that *these things don't happen* is incorrect.

Postscript: After having my DNA tested recently and looking at a family tree, I discovered that Edward's name was actually "Albert Edward" and Maria's name was "Martha Maria" but to their family and friends they were known as Edward and Maria. For anyone thinking that Isabelle had somehow discovered that I had "another family" or that super-psi had enabled her to psychically tap into the birth, marriage and death records, this pretty much rules that out and for me strengthens the evidence.

For the record, I'm definitely not suggesting anyone induce a head trauma or pay a visit to a medium, but for me, these experiences have been life-changing and for the better.

Back to the book.

*Our scientific power has outrun our spiritual power.
We have guided missiles and misguided men.*

~ *Martin Luther King, Jr.*

INTRODUCTION

In 1947, with the world shaken by the death toll of two global wars, a Doomsday Clock was created as a symbol of the likelihood of a global manmade catastrophe such as a nuclear war. The clock was originally set at seven minutes to midnight, midnight being the end of the world, at least, as we know it today.

The clock is maintained by the Bulletin of the Atomic Scientists' Science and Security Board,[6] a group of scientists and thinkers who monitor sciences, technology and anything that could be a global threat to humanity. As of January 2018 the clock is set to two minutes to midnight.

During the past month, President Trump has announced that the USA is pulling out of the long-standing Intermediate-Range Nuclear Forces (INF) Treaty citing Russia's development of weapons, which allegedly breach that agreement.

Some commentators think Trump's departure from the thirty-one year old treaty will increase the likelihood of a nuclear war with Russia, while others insist America needs to increase its nuclear capability to counter the rising military might of China.

Meanwhile, 5,500 miles from Washington DC, in Sochi, Russia, President Putin recently delivered his annual speech and added to the brouhaha when he said: "Only when we become convinced that there is an incoming attack on the territory of Russia, and that happens within seconds, only after that we would launch a retaliatory strike." He continued: "The aggressor should know that retaliation is inevitable, and he will be destroyed. ... We would be victims of an aggression and would get to heaven as martyrs, while those who initiated the aggression would just die and not even have time to repent."

In the secular West, church congregations might be in decline but more than a hundred years since the philosopher Friedrich Nietzsche declared, "God is dead," it seems the Lord is still evoked by leaders when they feel the need to justify their actions.

Speaking of evoking God, a movie is screening in American theaters. *The Trump Prophecy* is about retired firefighter Mark Taylor, who, while having treatment for PTSD in 2011, claimed he received a message from God telling him that Donald Trump would be the next president. The message began: "I've chosen this man Donald Trump for such a time as this. For, as Benjamin Netanyahu is to Israel, so shall this man be to the United States of America, for I will use this man to bring honor, respect and restoration to America."

Mark isn't the first person to claim to deliver a message from God, although, as far as I know, as a rule,

INTRODUCTION

God doesn't appear to pick leaders, at least not since the days of the Old Testament and Muhammad.

For thousands of years messages purporting to come from dimensions beyond our physical experience have been reported by deceased people *who are not* claiming to be God, via mystics, priests, mediums, shamen, near-death experiencers, ayahuasca drinkers, psychedelic drug takers, channelers, lucid dreamers, out-of-body experiencers, remote viewers, psychic sensitives and ordinary people.

During the first half of the twentieth century, with the advent and aftermath of two world wars, dead soldiers, airmen, and sailors were reportedly lining up in the astral[7] trying to get through to the living to let us know they had survived their physical deaths ... and the messages keep on coming to this day.

Having passed the hundred-year anniversary of the end of World War I, we could be forgiven for wondering if we will experience World War III in our lifetimes. Given the rhetoric from the leaders of certain nations and the media, it will be remarkable if we don't.

Why all this anger and fear-based politics? What are people afraid of? Many people's biggest fear seems to be losing control of their lives and dying. I can empathize with the fear of losing control of one's life. I recently watched both my parents suffer strokes, and, in events lasting not more than a few minutes, they both permanently lost control of their mental and physical lives—just like that.

A fear of loss of control or injury might be a good thing. It might stop us from walking across the street and getting hit by a truck. It might encourage us to live healthier lives in order to stave off self-inflicted debilitating illnesses. But why the fear of death? Birth and death are the most natural things we ever do. Many of us go to sleep every night without worrying about not waking up, so is the fear of death that many experience, a fear of what might happen *after* death? For some it definitely is and that's understandable. Two thousand years of being told we are going to the "good place" or the "bad place" must have had a conscious and unconscious influence on what we think and what we do.

Maybe we should pay more attention to some of these alleged after-death communications, if only to help us to navigate the post-death state when the time comes. If there's nothing, as atheists proclaim, ... no harm done.

What happens after we die? It's a natural question, because if we conclude that we continue to exist in some form, then the next question might be, do our thoughts and actions *here* influence our continued existence *there*? All religions say they do to a varying degree.

Is there a heaven and hell? And what of the purgatorial state that so many Christians reject? If there is nothing we'll never know, but if having died, we find ourselves aware of our continued existence, it might be useful to hear what others, who claim to have experienced death and who tell us they are further along the path, have to say.

There have been many accounts from people who claimed to have died in battle and *lived* to tell the tale. Their experiences are especially interesting because most have died as a result of violence and they often paint a vivid picture of their post-death state—their bodily state, if we can call it that—their psychological state and their subsequent philosophical worldview.

Can we trust what the communicators tell us? Who knows? Why do we trust some people and not others? We just do. Some Christians don't like the idea of

INTRODUCTION

after-death communication, possibly because the author of "Leviticus" in the Old Testament said: "Do not turn to mediums or seek out spiritists, for you will be defiled by them. I am the LORD your God" (Leviticus 19:31). After all, who wants to be defiled? But in the New Testament Jesus reportedly said: "Beloved, do not believe every spirit, but test the spirits to see whether they are from God, for many false prophets have gone out into the world" (1 John 4), and Jesus again: "Beware of false prophets, who come to you in sheep's clothing, but inwardly they are ravenous wolves. You will know them by their fruits" (Matthew 7:15-20).

In life we tend to test others to see if we trust them and we judge them by their words and actions. *We know them by their fruits.*

What follows is a collection of accounts written down by a variety of individuals, some notable, all seemingly sincere, who took the time to delve into the compelling world of after-death communication.

~ J. Beecher, Guildford,
United Kingdom. November 12, 2018.

*One great truth has become my constant companion.
I sum it up thus: Empty yourself if you would be filled.*

~ Private Dowding

1
PRIVATE DOWDING

Wellesley Tudor Pole

Major Wellesley Tudor Pole OBE, a.k.a. TP, (23 April 1884 – 13 September 1968) was an English writer, philosopher and mystic. He authored many essays and books and was a life-long spiritual truth seeker, being particularly involved with Spiritualism and a movement devoted to preserving the Chalice Well[8] and Bride's Mound of Glastonbury, England.

On a visit to Istanbul (then known as Constantinople) prior to the Young Turk Revolution in 1908, he heard of `Abdu'l-Bahá head of the Bahá'í Faith.

In November 1910 TP met `Abdu'l-Bahá and had the privilege of interviewing him over a nine day period in

Cairo and Alexandria. The meeting must have had a profound effect on Tudor Pole, because he embraced the faith and for the following decades he would remain active in the Bahá'í Faith.[9]

While a major in the British army, Tudor Pole (in collaboration with Sir Winston Churchill) came up with the idea for "The Silent Minute"[10] which TP claimed was divinely inspired, and for a period during World War II, all over Britain and the Commonwealth, millions of people joined together on certain evenings at 9.00 p.m. just before the news, to the chimes of Big Ben, to pray for peace.

Tudor Pole remarked at the time: "There is no power on earth that can withstand the united cooperation on spiritual levels of men and women of goodwill everywhere. It is for this reason that the continued and widespread observance of the Silent Minute is of such vital importance in the interest of human welfare."

In 1917 he wrote *Private Dowding: The personal story of a soldier killed in battle.* In the introduction below, Tudor Pole explains how this encounter with a deceased entity who called himself Private Dowding, was his first experience of clairvoyantly inspired automatic writing.

Introduction

On Monday, 12th March 1917, I was walking by the sea when I felt the presence of someone. I looked round; no one was in sight. All that day I felt as if someone were following me, trying to reach my thoughts. Suddenly I said to myself, "It's a soldier. He has been killed in battle and wants to communicate."

That evening I happened to call upon a lady who possesses some degree of clairvoyant power. I had forgotten about the soldier, until she described a man dressed in khaki, sitting in a chair near me. He was gazing intently in my direction. She said he was mature, wore a small moustache, and seemed somewhat sad. Not a very intelligent character apparently, but an honest one. I came home and sat down at my writing-table. Immediately my pen moved. Did I move it? Yes, in an involuntary sort of way. The thoughts were not my own; the language was a little unusual. Ideas were mainly conveyed in short simple phrases. It would really seem as if some intelligence outside myself were speaking through my mind and my pen.

Some of the ideas are not in conformity with preconceived notions of my own. The messages I received in this manner from "Thomas Dowding," recluse, schoolmaster, soldier, are set down exactly as they reached me.

Wellesley Tudor Pole
Bournemouth
20th March 1917

The Wilderness
12th March 1917, 9 p.m.

I am grateful for this opportunity. You may not realize how much some of us long to speak to those we have left behind. It is not easy to get messages through with certainty. They are so often lost in transit or misinterpreted. Sometimes the imagination of the receiver weaves a curious fabric round the thoughts we try to pass down, then the ideas we want to communicate are either lost or disfigured.

I was a schoolmaster in a small East Coast town before the war. I was an orphan, somewhat of a recluse, and I made friends but slowly. My name is of no importance; apparently names over here are not needed. I became a soldier in the autumn of 1915, and left my narrow village life behind. These details, however, are really of no importance. They may act as a background to what I have to say.

I joined as a private and died as a private. My soldiering lasted just nine months, eight of which were spent training in Northumberland. I went out with my battalion to France in July 1916 and we went into the trenches almost at once. I was killed by a shell splinter one evening in August and I believe that my body was buried the following day. As you see, I hasten over these unimportant events, important to me once, but now of no real consequence. How we overestimate the significance of earthly happenings. One only realizes this when freed from earthly ties.

Well, my body soon became cannon fodder, and there were few to mourn me. It was not for me to play anything but an insignificant part in this world-tragedy, which is still unfolding.

I am still myself, a person of no importance, but I feel I should like to say a few things before passing along. I feared death, but then that was natural. I was timid, and even feared life and its pitfalls. So I was afraid of being killed and was sure it would mean extinction. There are still many who believe that. It is because extinction has not come to me that I want to speak to you. May I describe my experiences? Perhaps they may prove useful to some. How necessary that some of us should speak back across the border! The barriers must be broken down. This is one of the ways of doing it. Listen, therefore, to what I have to say; physical death is nothing. There really is no cause for fear.

Some of my pals grieved for me. When I "went West" they thought I was dead for good. This is what happened. I have a perfectly clear memory of the whole incident. I was waiting at the corner of a traverse to go on guard. It was a fine evening. I had no special intimation of danger, until I heard the whizz of a shell. Then followed an explosion, somewhere behind me. I crouched down involuntarily, but was too late. Something struck, hard, hard, hard, against my neck. Shall I ever lose the memory of that hardness? It is the only unpleasant incident that I can remember. I fell and, as I did so, without passing through an apparent interval of unconsciousness, I found myself outside myself! You see I am telling my story simply; you will find it easier to understand. You will learn to know what a small incident this dying is.

Think of it! One moment I was alive, in the earthly sense, looking over a trench parapet, unalarmed, normal. Five seconds later I was standing outside my body, helping two of my pals to carry my body down the trench labyrinth towards a dressing station. They thought I was senseless but alive. I did not know whether I had jumped out of my body through shell shock, temporarily or forever. You see what a small thing is death, even the violent death of war!

I seemed in a dream. I had dreamt that someone or something had knocked me down. Now I was dreaming that I was outside my body. Soon I should wake up and find myself in the traverse waiting to go on guard. It all happened so simply. Death for me was a simple experience: no horror, no long-drawn suffering, no conflict. It comes to many in the same way. My pals need not fear death. Few of them do; nevertheless there is an underlying dread of possible extinction. I dreaded that; many soldiers do, but they rarely have time to think about such things. As in my case, thousands of soldiers pass over without knowing it.

If there be shock, it is not the shock of physical death. Shock comes later when comprehension dawns; "Where is my body? Surely I am not dead!' In my own case, I knew nothing more at the time than I have already related.

When I found that my two pals could carry my body without my help I dropped behind. I just followed, in a curiously humble way. Humble? Yes, because I seemed so useless. We met a stretcher party. My body was hoisted on to the stretcher. I wondered when I should get back into it again. You see I was so little "dead" that I imagined I was still (physically) alive. Think of it a moment before we pass on. I had been struck by a shell splinter. There was no pain. The life was knocked out of my body ... again, I say, there was no pain. Then I found that the whole of myself—all, that is, that thinks and sees and feels and knows—was still alive and conscious! I had begun a new chapter of life. I will tell you what I felt like. It was as if I had been running hard until, hot and breathless and I had thrown my overcoat away. The coat was my body and if I had not thrown it away I should have suffocated. I cannot describe the experience in a better way; there is nothing else to describe.

My body went to the first dressing station, and after examination was taken to a mortuary. I stayed near it all that night, watching, but without thoughts. It was as if my being, feeling, and thinking had become "suspended" by some power outside myself. This sensation came over me gradually as the night advanced. I still expected to wake up in my body again, that is, so far as I expected anything. Then I lost consciousness and slept soundly.

No detail seems to have escaped me. When I awoke, my body had disappeared! How I hunted and hunted! It began to dawn upon me that something strange had happened, although I still felt I was in a dream and should soon awake. My body had been buried or burned, I never knew which. Soon I ceased hunting for it. Then the shock came! It came without warning suddenly. I had been killed by a German shell! I was dead! I was no longer alive. I had been killed, killed, killed! Curious that I felt no shock when I was first driven outside my body. Now the shock came, and it was very real. I tried to think backwards, but my memory was numb (it returned later).

How does it feel to be "dead?" One can't explain, because there's nothing in it! I simply felt free and light. My being seemed to have expanded. These are mere words. I can only tell you just this: that death is nothing unseemly or shocking. So simple is the "passing along" experience that it beggars description. Others may have other experiences to relate of a more complex nature. I don't know.

When I lived in a physical body I never thought much about it. My health was fair. I knew very little about physiology. Now that I am living under other conditions I remain incurious as to that through which I express myself. By this I mean that I am still evidently in a body of some sort, but "I" can tell you very little about it. It has no interest for me. It is convenient, does not ache or tire, and seems similar in formation to my old body. There is a subtle difference, but I cannot attempt analysis.

Let me relate my first experience after I had somewhat recovered from the shock of realizing I was "dead." I was on, or rather above, the battlefield. It seemed as if I were floating in a mist that muffled sound and blurred the vision. Through this mist slowly penetrated a dim picture and some very low sounds. It was like looking through the wrong end of a telescope. Everything was distant, minute, misty and unreal. Guns were being fired. It might all have been millions of miles away. The detonation hardly reached me; I was conscious of the shells bursting without actually seeing them. The ground seemed very empty. No soldiers were visible. It was like looking down from above the clouds, yet that doesn't exactly express it either. When a shell that took [my] life exploded, then the sensation of it came much nearer to me. The noise and tumult came over the borderline with the lives of the slain. A curious way of putting it. All this time I was very lonely. I was conscious of none near me. I was neither in the world of matter nor could I be sure I was in any place at all! Just simply conscious of my own existence in a state of dream. I think I fell asleep for the second time, and long remained unconscious and in a dreamless condition.

At last I awoke. Then a new sensation came to me. It was as if I stood on a pinnacle, all that was essential of me. The rest receded, receded, receded. All appertaining to bodily life seemed to be dropping away down into a bottomless abyss. There was no feeling of irretrievable loss. My being seemed both minute and expansive at the same time. All that was not really me slipped down and away. The sense of loneliness deepened.

I do not find it easy to express myself. If the ideas are not clear, that is not your fault. You are setting down just what I impress upon you. How do I know this? I cannot see your pen, but I see my ideas as they are caught up and whirled into form within your mind. By "form" perhaps I mean words. Others may not feel this loneliness. I cannot tell whether my experiences are common to many in a like position. When I first "awoke" this second time, I felt cramped. This is passing and a sense of real freedom comes over me. A load has dropped away from me. I think my new faculties are now in working order. I can reason and think and feel and move. Once I read a book about this afterlife. It spoke of "planes" and "bodies" and "cycles" and "auras." I think a man named Sinnett or Symons wrote it. It purported to deal with the history and geography of this afterlife. I cannot confirm its descriptions from my own experience. I am simply myself, alive, in a region where food and drink seem unnecessary. Otherwise "life" is strangely similar to earth life. A "continuation," but with more freedom. I have no more to say just now. Will you let me return another time and use your mind again? I shall be so grateful.

13th March 1917, 8 pm.

You are kind to me. You loan me a power I do not possess any longer—the power to convey information to my human fellows on earth. I can use your mind freely because I see you have deliberately chained your imagination, and so I can impress you freely and clearly.

From this you may notice that I am a little farther along my new road. I have been helped. Also I have recovered from the "shock," not of my transition but of my recognition of it. This is no subtlety—it is simply what I mean. I am no longer alone—I have met my dear brother. He came out here three years ago and has come down to welcome me. The tie between us is strong. William could not get near me for a long time, he says. The atmosphere was so thick. He hoped to reach me in time to avert the "shock" to which I have referred but found it impossible.

He is working among the newly arrived and has wide experience. A good deal of what follows came to me from him; I have made it my own, and so can pass it on. You see, I am still possessed with the desire to make my experience, my adventure, of help to others who have not yet arrived here.

It appears that there are rest halls in this region, specially prepared for newly arrived pilgrims. I shall use your language. We can only convey our experiences approximately. To describe conditions here in words is quite impossible. Please remember this. My brother helped me into one of these rest halls. Confusion at once dropped away from me. Never shall I forget my happiness. I sat in the alcove of a splendid domed hall. The splashing of a fountain reached my tired being and soothed me. The fountain "played" music, color, harmony and bliss. All discordancies vanished and I was at peace. My brother sat near me. He could not stay long, but promised to return. I wanted to find you at once to tell you I had found peace, but it is only now that I could do so. On earth, the study of crystal formations was a great hobby of mine. To my intense delight I discovered that this splendid hall was constructed according to the law of crystal formations. I spent hours in examining various parts of it. I shall spend hours and days and weeks there. I can continue my studies and make endless discoveries. What happiness! When I have regained a state of poise, my brother says I may help him in his work outside. I am in no hurry for this.

You evidently know nothing about crystals. I cannot impress your mind with the wonders of this place. What a pity! This place is so different from any earthly edifice that I fear it is useless to attempt description. As it is, people will say I am romancing. Or else they will say that you, my faithful scribe, have let your imagination run away with you. Please let me return again later. I still have much to say.

14th March 1917, 5 pm.

I am beginning to meet people and to exchange ideas. Strange that the only person I came across for a long time was my brother. He tells me that I have never been really alone. The mist around me, shutting me off, has emanated from myself, he says. This fact rather humiliates me. I suppose my loneliness of life and character whilst on earth has followed me here. I always lived in books—they were my real world. And, even then, my reading was technical rather than general.

I begin to see now that my type of mind would find itself isolated, or rather would emanate isolation, when loosed from earthly trammels. I shall remain near earth conditions whilst learning lessons I refused to learn before.

It is dangerous to live to and for oneself. Tell this to my fellows with emphasis. The life of a recluse is unwise, except for the very few who have special work that requires complete silence and isolation. I was not one of these. I cannot remember doing anything really worthwhile. I never looked outside myself.

My school? Well, teaching bored me. I simply did it to earn my bread and cheese. People will say I was unique, a crabby, selfish old bachelor. Selfish yes, but alas, far from being unique. I was thirty-seven when I came over here, that is ... my body was. Now I feel so ignorant and humble that I don't feel I've begun to have any age at all. I must dwell on this.

Live widely. Don't get isolated. Exchange thoughts and services. Don't read too much. That was my mistake. Books appealed to me more than life or people. I am now suffering for my mistakes. In passing on these details of my life I am helping to free myself.

What a good thing the war dragged me out into life! In those nine months I learned more about human nature than I had conceived possible. Now I am learning about my poor fossilized old self. It is a blessing I came here. Though I do not regret, I like to hear what is going on in the region you inhabit. It seems a long way off already. I told my brother I wanted news about events on earth. He took me to visit an old gentleman who had been editor of a newspaper. Why do I call him "old?" Because he died at eighty-one and has not thrown off earth conditions yet. He therefore surrounds himself with these conditions. His son on earth runs the paper, a French journal. The old man can read his son's thoughts and so divines the world's news through his son's mind. He has built himself an office, full of telephones and tape machines. These machines are in a way illusory, but they please the old gentleman. He received me courteously, and insisted on hearing details of my crossing. He was disappointed that I did not know his paper by name or reputation, and surprised that I knew so little about earthly affairs. "I want to get back," he said. "I cannot get along without my paper. My son often uses my ideas in his editorials without knowing it." This fact was the cause of much amusement to him. I asked him for some current news. This is what he told me:

> Something interesting is going on, for my son stays at the office all night. There is "war as usual." There is some commotion about food. I saw Guilbert writing an article for the paper on "World Shortage." England seems to be scared about it. They have suddenly remembered the existence of the land they are fighting for, and they are digging it about. Something must have stopped food supplies or destroyed them.
>
> Food seems more important now than shells. The rest of the world seems coming into the war at least, Guilbert thinks so.

I see an article headed "America and China." Are they short of food too, or are they to fight? I think they are going to side with France. Turkey must be having a bad time. I see the headline, "Turkish Debacle." Guilbert seems full of excitement about Russia. I see into his mind. He is evolving an article on "Russia: the Coming World Power." Russia must have won a big victory somewhere. Yes, I think the war is going on all right. Our circulation has increased again, but alas! Guilbert cannot get enough paper. I wish I were down there. I would have laid in a big stock months ago.

The old gentleman was still rambling on about his paper and its prospects when I came away. How awful to be chained to an earthly property like that! Tell people to control their worldly interests from outside, If you identify yourself heart and soul with some material project or undertaking, you will find it hanging on to you over here. It will obsess you, blot out the view, and make progress impossible. This old French editor came over a good many years ago.[11]

Then came the war; and I went with the rest,
To learn my lessons, with death as a guest,
The days and nights that I spent overseas,
The bombing of cities, of people, of trees ...
... that hell
Of hating and killing, of shot and shell...

~ Gertrude Tooley Buckingham

2

DEATH ON THE BATTLEFIELD

Lord Dowding

By 1940 World War II was raging, and one of the most prominent men in Great Britain was Air Chief Marshal Hugh Caswall Tremenheere Dowding, more widely known as Lord Dowding.[12] Dowding was the commander of RAF Fighter Command during the Battle of

Britain and played a crucial role in thwarting Hitler's plan to defeat Great Britain. In the 1969 film, *Battle of Britain,* Dowding was played by one of Britain's much loved actors, Laurence Olivier.

What is less well known is, after the Battle of Britain Dowding devoted the rest of his life to exploring life after death and what we now refer to as psychical research. He authored four books on the subject, *Many Mansions* (1943), *Lychgate* (1945), *The Dark Star* (1951), and *God's Magic* (1960).

After the war ended, Dowding was often contacted by mothers and loved ones of airmen who had died on his watch, and when he asked his local vicar how he should respond to their grieving, allegedly, the vicar replied nonchalantly, "Tell them they're with God." Not being content with the vicar's answer, Dowding continued his own investigation, in an attempt to find the truth to the age-old question, "What happens after we die?"

He read everything he could on life after death, reincarnation and Spiritualism. He sat regularly with mediums and for many years in a home circle, and naturally he came to his own conclusions on the subject.

In *Lychgate,* he gives an indication as to his thinking;

> To you I would say, "Read a little about Theosophy."[13] Now I want to make it quite clear that I am not a Theosophist, I am a Dowding-ist if I am any kind of an -ist at all. But I do believe that the Theosophists are nearer to the truth than any other Western creed or sect of which I have heard. I say this not so much because I trust my own power of judgment, but because the little doles of information from the other side, which we get in our circle from time to time, so often fit into the Theosophical picture, and into no other frame.

Dowding met many psychics and mediums during his investigations and claimed he was followed by a band of deceased airman who were drawn to him. In his books, the communication with the airmen are fascinating. Often funny, sometimes sad, but never dull, Dowding's writings are a must for anyone pondering the nature of existence and whether we survive physical death.

Here he documents examples of deceased soldiers coming to terms with their experiences after physical death.

∼

As a contrast to the somewhat sterile attempt to prove the facts of survival and communication by argument, I should like you to read the following messages, which have all come from men killed in action during the present war. They came to Mrs. Gascoigne and her daughter through the agency of the late Colonel Gascoigne[14] who is organizing the first spiritual contacts with those who die in battle. Colonel Gascoigne was with the force that was attempting to relieve Khartoum when it fell,[15] and he was also associated with Cecil Rhodes in the early days of Rhodesia.

Only two or three of the men had known the Gascoignes in life, but they were, so to speak, "introduced" by the Colonel. Most of the messages are contained in the last chapter of *The Triumph of Life Eternal*,[16] but a few are now published [here] for the first time.

From a sailor, the son of an old friend.

I was in an oil tanker and we were all drowned when she was hit. It was very quick and I did not suffer any pain but tremendous surprise at finding myself possessed of the most wonderful strength and able to heave away all kinds of wreckage. I was making my way through the debris when I realized that we were moving through deep water. It was so still that it was just like a dream. I remember feeling it was quite easy to move and there was no difficulty in breathing (if we were breathing), but now I come to think of it, it was a different sort of breath. Anyhow I got free and so did some of my friends and we moved away without quite knowing what we were doing. We found a stranger had joined us; his clothes were quite dry and he walked through the water without it seeming to touch him. I noticed this and, after a time, I said something to him about it.

It all seemed so queer, and as we walked and walked I saw that we were going towards what looked like a sunrise, the best I've ever seen, and I turned to look back over the way we had come, and the stranger put his hand on my shoulder and said: "Not yet, you must go on out of the Valley of the Shadow of Death and then you can return if you want to." I said, "Oh, I don't care," and I went on in a dazed sort of way until we came to a kind of garden, but it wasn't enclosed, it was on the hillside with lots and lots of flowers; oh, they were lovely. By this time I had realized that we were not walking in the water any more and I felt so tired and sleepy, and my feet refused to go any further, and the stranger suggested that we should rest. I sat down on the grass and was soon asleep.

You cannot imagine my astonishment on waking to find myself in a strange place, and I couldn't at first remember how I got there; but it came back after a time, and I found some of the others, and they let me piece it together with their help. But all the time the stranger stayed with us, and he listened but said nothing. So at last I asked him where he came from, and why he'd brought us here, and he said: "Oh, I'm just a seaman like you, but I've been ashore for some time now, so I thought I might be able to help you." Then, very slowly, we all knew that we were what we used to call "dead," but it was so different that I couldn't believe it.

It's grand, just GRAND. I wish my mother could know about it.

We are in a far better land than the one we left, and it's all okay. I'd love her to see it. Dad came to me soon after I realized this and we had a great time together. It seems queer to call him dad: he's younger than I am now; at least he looks it. We are to have a job together soon, but I am not to be in a hurry.

From a New Zealander.

Can I try? I do not find it difficult, but what is the use of trying? You do not know my people; they are far away and would never understand. I am one of the Colonial troops and my name is Simson. I came from New Zealand. I guess some of the lads have had their fill of fighting, but that was what we came for, and I am glad I came. I know it wasn't much use in the ordinary way, but we showed our loyalty to Britain, and that's the spirit that will prevail in the end. I was one of the casualties in Greece. I feel I should go home now, but I can't leave my mates. I could go as swiftly as a thought, and return equally quickly, but time doesn't matter now, and if I let go the contact with our lads I may find it difficult to pick it up again. I feel we can do something here now, and if that's so, let's go on doing it.

I am rather vague as to who is "alive" and who is "dead;" they all look much alike, but the "dead" are far more active and don't get tired. It seems strange, but I sort of expected this when I came over. I knew I should never go back alive. But my parents would never understand how much more alive I am now, so it's no use my trying to tell them.

I am going straight on with my job, under my own officer, and with many of my pals; we work for the rest, especially when they are asleep; sometimes we raid the enemy's "dead" battalion, fighting with our thought weapons! It's a grand game. There are so few things we can't do now. One of the strangest things is that we all feel happy. I wasn't one of the naturally happy ones on Earth. I worried and fidgeted and found time lagged more than most people. But here there is a sort of carefree feeling, and no time to lag, so I can't work up any regret over leaving my body. I stay right here. Our boys are happy, too, all of them, and the others are having such a rough time that it's up to us to stay by them.

Q. *Can we help you? Do you need our help?*

Well, yes, we do. It's ever such a help to do this; it kind of gives me more pep to get into closer touch with my pals. It would be much better if you could have a talk with more of us. You give us confidence.

So often we cannot see the result of our work, but now I can feel and see your reactions, and it makes real work, like I expect it does for you.

Something to show for it. Thank you ever so much. I think that's all for now. Goodnight.

~ Gunner Simson.

From a Norwegian.

Thank you. I feel rather strange doing this, but it goes quite easily. I am not English, nor even British: I am a Norwegian. I have lived in England for many years and I find your language as easy as mine own.

I was shot by the Germans in Trondheim. I was a little shopkeeper—they shoot. I do not love the Germans. I never shall, but I am held up here by my hatred. I find that I cannot throw it off. I still feel so angry for their acts of unprovoked cruelty, and I am consumed with my passionate anger and cannot get free. I beg of you to help me—your father, [Colonel Gascoigne] he brings me to you to make a closer link with him. He tell me that we must forgive the Nazis, that they do not know what they do, that they are like sleep-walkers, and until I forgive them I cannot get free, to pass from this plane so near the Earth on to other planes.

Here all that happens with you is known and felt in a greater form, and we go on feeling more and more animosity against the German race, and when they join us in the astral body we feel far more antagonism than we felt during our Earth life. It is awful, this anger that we cannot shake it off. Give me serenity and let me sleep. I want to sleep and forget them. I might be fairer in my judgment and come to forgive.

I see why Christ quickly forgave everyone before he left his earth body. I see the reason and the need, and with the help of your father and this contact that you have given me, I shall escape.

~ J. AMMUSSEN.

IN TIMES OF WAR

A Highlander taken prisoner in Crete.

Yes, I was in Crete. I'm a Highlander. I was in the Marines and I stayed on in Crete among those who couldn't be taken off. It was one of the worst moments when I saw the ships and knew it was hopeless for us to hope for any escape. I got hit in the shoulder, and there was nothing for it but to give in and let them take me prisoner. I was put on to a stretcher and taken to hospital, but they did nothing for me except to give me a bed to lie on, and my wound got septic and very painful. I got delirious I suppose, and they came and questioned me, but I don't think they did anything for me. Perhaps they couldn't; I don't know. Anyway, after ages and ages of suffering I seemed to pass into a timeless sleep, and when I woke up there was no pain, and I was out of doors, so I thought I had escaped and I wandered about glad to be free, but I couldn't make sense of it all. I seemed unable to walk properly, I couldn't keep on the ground, and though I didn't fall it was extremely difficult to move along, and then the whole place would grow misty; I would see places and people one moment and the next I saw something quite different. I thought I was delirious again. Now I know that I was seeing two planes at once, and I hadn't learnt to manage my spirit body. It all worried me a lot and I got quite hopeless. People would come up to help me, and just as we were beginning to understand each other I would see the outline of Crete, and be overcome by the desire to hide away from the Germans, it was a sort of torture, and then at last they got through to me and I was able to sleep—the real sleep of death—the putting off of our life and the taking on of another. I don't know much about it, but this life seems so natural that I was anxious to try and write through you so as to test my power on the physical plane before going back to help those who have suffered like I did. I know we can and I don't want to waste time. It's grand finding that nothing was wasted.

I have all the faculties now that I longed to have on earth. Oh, it's simply grand. Goodnight.

From a Polish pilot who spent his last leave with us.

Yes, I am shot down and out. I have survived many fights, but not this one. I am wounded. I cannot control the aircraft; it was my leg, you feel the pain. I could not move the controls and I fall. I cannot leave the aircraft. I fall quite consciously. I get up without any pain. I see my observer and gunner: he is hurt, too, but not so much. The Germans come to find us. They do not see me. I run and hide, but they not look for me; my friend they take away. I wander about. I feel well and cannot think how I came to crash aircraft. My leg is healed. I wander about. I go to the French peasants and ask for help, but they do not see me, and I begin to wonder. I am neither hungry nor thirsty nor particularly tired.

I begin to see things changing—I see first colors everywhere; it is sunset, or sunrise, and it looks as if the colors were reflected in the earth as well as in the sky. I lay and watched the color take form; it was like a cinema when one picture fades out and another takes its place. I was astounded. I do not know where I am. I ask; I pray; I forget that I have no faith in religion. I pray for help and it comes to me. Someone looking very strange and yet quite like ourselves comes to me: he tells me not to mind the change—it is best for all and that I shall be happy in this land.

I am very confused. I think I am taken prisoner, then he explains that there are no prisons or prisoners and I feel free again. He took me away and he told me to sleep; he touched my eyes and I sleep at once. When I wake he is still there and I am on earth again in the occupied territory with Germans all round. I have come back to my body. I find it difficult to leave it.

I see no colors, but my new friend is there too, and he talks to me, but I can't see him well. They are doing something to my body. I am miserable, so my friend tells me to think very hard of some place outside the war, so I think very hard of the last time I see family life with you at H—. I see you all quite easily, and I wake you and you feel me near and you talk to me. I ask you to let me stay and just sit quietly in your house far from the battle until I can go on, and you say, "Yes," so I stay, and now I begin to feel sleepy again. I am between the worlds—help me to throw off this one and to go on. I want to go on ... I want to go on. I think I can; please help me.

~ S. Z.

Several days later.

Thank you, yes I am well. I do not yet feel ready to leave your home for very long at a time, but I go for a short time, but it is good to come back to you all. I have strange feelings when you sit in the same chair in which I sit. I am close and yet not close at all.

I am going now sometimes to Poland, but I dare not stay. I have no strength yet to help them, and they need this power so badly. I see my old friends, some dying and some dead, but I can do nothing. I am tired and feel too ill to reach them. We must help soon, but at present we are too weak.

Your father, or someone like, he comes with me and we try to help but I am nearly useless. I want to help but I am like a child, I cannot.

Also, I never had any faith, nothing to expect on dying, and I am lost; I know nothing. All the things I made fun of come back to me. I was a bad man. I neglected many things, my prayers and my church, but I do not know if that mattered. I had no creed, and now I find that extinction being impossible I have to suffer a sort of conscious extinction, knowing and feeling, and yet being empty of strength.

What you expect here, that you find—you build your awakening, it is just as you imagined, at least that is what they told me. I expected nothing, so nothing came. But now I am pulling out of the difficult doldrums, and am beginning to feel my strength. Thank you for helping.

~ S. Z.

From a Tank Officer.

Thank you. I am alive after all. I thought extinction was the only thing that could follow such an inferno. We seemed to go down on all sides British and German alike, tanks, guns and planes. I had the feeling that we were being exterminated by the machines of our own creation—they seemed so much stronger and more vindictive than the humans inside them. I believe it's the battle of the machines; they are in charge and we are the slaves of some evil genius through whom they have been created. I feel the influence of evil so strongly—I longed to get away and lie in the clean sand and forget the horrors of man's inferno of which we did not seem to be in charge.

I prayed for help when we were stuck in the sand and fire broke out, and I prayed with all my soul and I knew we couldn't escape, but prayer seemed to strengthen me and I felt that nothing really mattered so desperately, excepting the feeling of evil, and that had receded. I could not name it or explain it in words. It seemed to meet us from the sand and hang all around the tank battle. I felt sick and miserable, and then it passed off and I found myself standing outside the tank talking to my Colonel. He seemed unconscious of the bullets that were raining down upon us. I ran for shelter but he called me and told me not to bother. He was looking as young as a subaltern and as though he was enjoying the battle.

He took me by the shoulder and said: "Don't you see, Kit, we are dead, and yet far more alive than they are, and we can go on fighting, hampering the enemy, throwing dust in his eyes, putting ideas into our leaders and playing an invisible hand." I saw that he was serious but I thought he was mad, I said: "Yes, Sir, but I'm so tired I don't think I can move any further." He left me and I don't know what happened, but I woke up here with only one idea—to go back to the battle and find him. He wasn't mad, but I was stupid.

Your father has let me write through you so as to give me the strength from the physical plane to grapple with the unseen world. I'm off now. Thanks a lot.

February 4th, 1942.

Here are two people who would like to write:
Yes, I am very glad to have this chance. I always thought it might be so, but until I was picked off by a Jap sniper, I was never certain.

DEATH ON THE BATTLEFIELD

I fell face downwards in the swampy mud of the jungle, and lay unconscious for a time in a sort of nightmare: my body was trying to reassert itself and my spirit to get free. Never think that when people are unconscious that they are really so, at least I wasn't. It was a time of conscious paralysis. I hated it, and, when something snapped and I was free, I was awfully relieved.

I got back to our fellows and I soon realized what had happened when they didn't see me; but I was so interested in finding myself unchanged that I hadn't time to think of anything else. I wanted to tell them not to fear death and all that but I couldn't. After a time I began to see the Jap dead. They were helping their own fellows, and the living Japs could sometimes see and hear them, and they used all the information given, and this made me feel that we should be able to do the same. I tried awfully hard, but I couldn't warn or suggest anything which could be accepted by the brains of our fellows, so I wandered off wondering what to do next.

I didn't exactly want to leave them to it, but there didn't seem to be any alternative, so I did. I wandered off into the forest, and for a time forgot all about the war, and all that my friends were going through because I became so fascinated by the life that I saw all around me. I know the jungle well. I have lived in it, alone, for months on end, and I came back to it seeking rest and peace after the turmoil of war, and I found all I sought and more, much more. I suddenly found that I was seeing things that had been hidden from me during the whole of my physical life. I cannot describe the beauty of the life around me. The jungle is always rich in color, sound and beauty of trees and flowers, but now behind each thing that I knew so well lurked a hidden meaning, and some beautiful ray or sound seemed to permeate the very texture of the jungle life.

I can't explain. I was superbly happy and entirely myself, but that self had grown in comprehension, and in power to experience contentment and bliss.

Then a voice came to my ears, and gradually I sensed a beautiful shining figure that said to me: "Here you see the land of pure content, but you have left behind a land of passionate unrest. Do you not wish to help others to find the key to this place of joy?" I was so overcome at never having thought of anyone else for ages, that I must have blushed like a schoolboy, but the Shining One didn't seem to notice. So I stammered that I hadn't really grasped my whereabouts yet, and could he help me? He said: "No, you found the way, and the rest you must discover for yourself, but others may not be so fortunate and need helping." I didn't want to turn my back on this glorious place, but the Shining One promised to come with me and not leave me. He explained that I could always return just by recalling this place vividly and wishing myself here, and now, equally, you and I must see ourselves in the battle zone.

I did most regretfully, and away we seemed to pass, or rather there was no passing, one surrounding faded out and another took shape. The jungle moved or dissolved and its place was taken by another sort of jungle full of men shouting orders and screaming in pain. I felt unable to bear it at first, but the Shining One said: "Come and stand by this man, he is about to pass over to us." A second later and a bullet had ripped through his stomach and he lay groaning at our feet. The Shining One bent down, and touched his head and eyes, and instantly the groaning ceased, and I saw his spirit leave his tortured body, and, looking dazed and pale, joined us both in the deep foliage of the jungle. Before I knew what had happened we were back in the wonderful jungle; it was a delicious experience. The man who had joined us was one of our own men. A dull, quiet looking fellow. I hardly knew him; he took no interest in games and was always reading. Now he brightened up suddenly upon catching sight of me, and said: "Hello, Sir, I didn't think you'd be here. I thought I'd seen you killed some days ago." I said: "Yes, and I saw you killed some minutes ago." The Shining One looked at me and I knew I shouldn't have broken the news so swiftly. But Burrows didn't seem to mind, "Oh, well, I've copped it have I? Well, I don't care, it's awful fighting here and not much chance of getting out," was all he said. "But what's it like here?" he continued.

I told him it was splendid, and that he had nothing to fear, and we walked about through the jungle clearing while the Shining One explained things to us. Soon we had both recovered from the shock and he took us back to the firing line to fetch more of our people and introduce them to this life. That is where we are now, and I wanted to get further and learn how to impress my thoughts upon the men in charge.

I'm grateful to you for my first lesson—it doesn't seem to have gone too badly, but I'm tired now and I'll wish myself back in my jungle home of refreshment. I see there are no separate places and all are moods within ourselves, just like what we were taught as children. "The Kingdom of God is within you." Goodnight.

A message from Libya:

O. K., I am glad. I've wanted to thank you for some time but I couldn't make you hear.

We came abroad in the spring. I was one of the Snodsbury lot. I'll give you my name soon but you likely don't remember me. We was all split up and I got sent to

Egypt. It was a show … I never thought as how I could have lived through it. You know what I mean. I didn't know that dying was like this. I thought it was all over and finished and sometimes we seemed to go through such a grueling, I didn't see as how we could stand any more, and then, all of a sudden, it ceased and I was feeling as upright as a trivet. A moment before I'd been dead beat and hot; oh, hot and thirsty with the most awful headache. The noise of battle fairly shattered me to bits, but then, all of a sudden, I was cool and fit and fresh as a daisy, and perky as could be, just looking on and hearing the noise, but not feeling shattered by it. I couldn't believe I was a "gonner." I saw my body just holed all over, and yet I couldn't believe it. I think I tried to pull it away from the gun, but there were others on top and beside me all in a heap. We'd got a direct hit all right.

The rest weren't there; that seemed queer to me, none of them, until I saw the officer. He came up to me, I pointed to where his body lay, and he gave a kind of gasp and said, "Oh, well, I suppose that's that; it's a queer world, Johnson, and I suppose we'd best carry on." I says, "Yes, Sir, but wot does we do now?"

"Load the gun of course, you blighter," ses he, just as he used to. I went to obey, but strong as I felt I could not move the shells. They weren't so heavy as all that, but I could not get a hold of them: they was slippery; it seemed as though there was a sort of fish scale between my fingers and the shells. I couldn't hold it. I tell the officer and he comes to help, cursing proper he was by this time, and the two of us had a go, but would she budge? Not an inch. It seemed silly like; there was us two great hefty fellows trying all we knew to lift one small ack-ack shell and we just couldn't do it. At last I sat down and laughed. "Well," I ses, "did you ever hear of two dead blokes firing a gun?"

"Yes, I did," ses he, all angry now and red in the face, "and, wot's more, we are going to do it. We are fit enough, aren't we? Come on." So I heaved to again, thinking he'd gone crazy but that it was better to humor him. So we tried again, and now I begun to see things—not the efforts we was making with our hands, if you follow me, but the Captain; he seemed to be sending out power some way, he was that determined, and I saw him as you might imagine a call-up station on the wireless (if you could see one) and the answer came not through his fingers but through himself.

Lots of shadowy people came round us and worked with us, and the gun wasn't exactly in action, but something was being fired from her.

Plane after plane came over, and suddenly lost speed, turned for home or crashed. I was mystified. I couldn't recollect anything like this: there seemed to be no noise, the discharge was silent, but the repercussion was distinctly felt by us all, and that seemed to give us fresh impetus for the next. It was the queerest experience. Just then I saw Jock coming towards us: he'd stopped a packet, too, but he hadn't been with us before.

He recognized me and the Captain, and saluted and stood ready for duty; the Captain was too busy to notice him and Jock was always one for arguing, so I shut him up with "Just you wait and see, Son, we're learning new operational tactics, us three gonners from the old batch, so come along and learn and don't interrupt, whatever you do." So I stayed close to Jock and made him watch the Captain.

The Captain was a grand fellow, not a doubt. He seemed to drive his way through with all his determination against it all, and, when I made to move, he looked up that sharp, and said: "You sit quiet and think, for God's sake think with all the guts you've got in you, that's what you must do now. We've got our brains and our determination and if we three hold together we'll pull it off and keep the air protection for our chaps. Don't you see the men who are helping us?" and then I looked and there was Sandy, who got sniped on Thursday, standing waist high in water, making strange movements with his arms. I looked at his eyes, and they were Sandy's, but different, so clear like stars, he seemed inspired, if one could say, so I don't think I can finish the story today. May I stop now, and come again? I've loved telling it to you. You see it's my first real adventure. Thank you.

JOHNSON.

Continuation from O. K.

O. K., I'm all right. I'd like ever so much to finish what I was saying.

Well, as I said, Sandy looked inspired. I can't think of another word, and all at once he seemed to be leading us, and not so much the officer who was following his orders most carefully, and, as the shadowy people became clearer, I seemed to lose touch with the live people, and the dead ones seemed more real. Then the Jerries attacked and took the gun and we weren't touched. He came through us without seeing or hearing us, though we could see and hear him and feel the perspiry sense of his nearness. I loathed the smell all of a sudden; though it was familiar enough, it almost made me sick, and I saw Sandy and the officer had moved away. So I pulled Jock up and said: "Don't let's lose sight of those two or we're lost." Jock agreed, but when I got to my feet I found I couldn't stay on the ground; it was most comical and so difficult to move on. I was kind of floating and so was Jock. I said: "Let's hold hands and keep each other down," but instead we seemed to buoy each other up. Oh, we did have a time catching up with Sandy and the Captain, but they didn't notice us; someone else had joined them. He wasn't in uniform and I wondered, for a minute, how a civilian could have got there; he looked like an Arab, and then, when he turned and looked at me, I felt—I felt as though he was re-making me all over again. I knelt down and murmured "Christ" with all the reverence of a child.

"No, not Christ, but a messenger from Him," said the man I was kneeling before, and "He wants you," that was what he said. He wanted me.

"Whatever for?" I gasped out, and I looked up to see where the others were, but I could see nothing but a blinding glorious light. It seemed to fill my head and burn through something that was keeping me there, and then the voice spoke again, something like this: "By your sacrifice you have attained to the Crown of Fortitude"—and then I remember no more.

That was the last I saw of earth. I'd like some of the chaps to know how we pass on: it's a most wonderful thing.

I'm tired now and can't finish.

Thank you.

JOHNSON.[17]

*There is no such thing as death; life is only a dream,
and we are the imagination of ourselves.*

~ Bill Hicks

3

NOT QUITE DEAD YET

So far, the examples in this book are of people who, having died, have allegedly made contact with the living in dreams, via mediums and by other psychic means such as automatic writing.[18]

Throughout our recorded history, people have come close to death or suffered severe physical or emotional trauma and reported having a near-death experience (NDE) or a spiritually transformative experience, (STE) where they sometimes meet beings, religious figures, pets and deceased friends and relatives, some of whom they weren't aware had passed away prior to their experience.

People who have been blind from birth claim to see for the first time. They report having an out-of-body experience and seeing medical personnel working on their *own* bodies in the operating theater.[19]

Some, like me, remember nothing of the event but retain all the after-effects. I was at a "Beyond the Brain" conference in London in 2018 where Diane Corcoran, R.N., Ph.D., a US army colonel, now retired, was one of the speakers.

Diane became aware of NDEs before the term was coined, while working as an army nurse on the battlefields of Vietnam. Since that time she has been president of the board of the International Association for Near-Death Studies (IANDS), working to help veterans deal with their experiences. Diane states that many soldiers, particularly those who suffer a head injury, experience the after-effects of an NDE or STE *but have no memory of the event itself.*

Doctors often assume that these patients are suffering from PTSD or some other medical condition, whereas NDEs and STEs can be transformative events if only they are recognised as such. Diane talked about soldiers returning home from war and giving their money away. Typically they no longer have any interest in cars, money, stuff or other materialistic pursuits. They change their careers for something more altruistic; they end relationships, become more attuned to nature, take up voluntary work, become pacifists, and often they have no idea why they're doing these things. Family and friends struggle because they feel they're dealing with a different person, which in a way, they are.[20]

In an interview with *Moon* magazine Diane cites one example:

> One man drove four hundred miles to talk with me and he said, "There's something wrong with me. I

can't watch television. I cry at commercials. I used to love boxing, but I can't watch it anymore. There's just so much violence and commercialism everywhere. There's nowhere I can go to be at peace."[21]

I completely empathize with that man.

In 1990, the Australian media tycoon, Kerry Packer,[22] suffered a heart attack while playing polo in Sydney. After being clinically dead for six to seven minutes he recovered and later famously said; "I've been to the other side and let me tell you, son, there's fucking nothing there. There's no one waiting there for you ... there's no one to judge you so you can do what you bloody well like."

Kerry's statement is understandable, because like the majority of people who recover from cardiac arrest, he didn't have an NDE or any kind of experience. But according to ever increasing data being gathered around the world, between 4% and 15% of adults do have an experience, irrespective of whether they are atheists, Christians, Hindus, Buddhists, Muslims, new agers or otherwise. Interestingly, when it comes to children, that percentage rises dramatically; IANDS[23] reports, "About 85% of children who experience cardiac arrest have an NDE."

The term near-death experience entered the mainstream in the 1970s when psychologist Raymond Moody coined the phrase in his landmark book, *Life After Life*. In that book, Moody interviewed 150 people who had experienced the near-death phenomenon. These days there are thousands of examples on a number of online forums around the world.[24]

The Vision of Er

One of the earliest near-death experiences recorded is "The Vision of Er"[25] reported by the philosopher Plato during his dialogue with Socrates in book ten of *Republic* written in 360 BC.

Er was ostensibly killed in battle but, after twelve days, he woke up on a funeral pyre and told a story of his journey into the afterlife.

Socrates[26] tells the story, thus:

> "Well, I said, I will tell you a tale; not one of the tales which Odysseus tells to the hero Alcinous, yet this too is a tale of a hero, Er the son of Armenius, a Pamphylian by birth. He was slain in battle, and, ten days afterwards, when the bodies of the dead were taken up already in a state of corruption, his body was found unaffected by decay, and carried away home to be buried. And on the twelfth day, as he was lying on the funeral pile, he returned to life and told them what he had seen in the other world. He said that when his soul left the body he went on a journey with a great company, and that they came to a mysterious place at which there were two openings in the earth; they were near together, and over against them were two other openings in the heaven above.

> "In the intermediate space there were judges seated, who commanded the just, after they had given judgment on them and had bound their sentences in front of them, to ascend by the heavenly way on the right hand; and in like manner the unjust were bidden by them to descend by the lower way on the left hand; these also bore the symbols of their

deeds, but fastened on their backs. He drew near, and they told him that he was to be the messenger who would carry the report of the other world to men, and they bade him hear and see all that was to be heard and seen in that place. Then he beheld and saw on one side the souls departing at either opening of heaven and earth when sentence had been given on them; and at the two other openings other souls, some ascending out of the earth dusty and worn with travel, some descending out of heaven clean and bright.

"And arriving ever and anon they seemed to have come from a long journey, and they went forth with gladness into the meadow, where they encamped as at a festival, and those who knew one another embraced and conversed, the souls which came from earth curiously enquiring about the things above, and the souls which came from heaven about the things beneath. And they told one another of what had happened by the way, those from below weeping and sorrowing at the remembrance of the things which they had endured and seen in their journey beneath the earth (now the journey lasted a thousand years), while those from above were describing heavenly delights and visions of inconceivable beauty. The story, Glaucon, would take too long to tell but the sum was this: He said that for every wrong which they had done to any one they suffered tenfold; or once in a hundred years, such being reckoned to be the length of man's life, and the penalty being thus paid ten times in a thousand years. If, for example, there were any who had been the cause of many deaths, or had betrayed or enslaved cities or armies, or been guilty of any other evil behavior, for each and all of their offences they received punishment ten times over, and the rewards of beneficence and justice and holiness were in the same proportion. I need hardly repeat what he said concerning young children dying almost as soon as they were born. Of piety and impiety to gods and parents, and of murderers, there were retributions other and greater far which he described. He mentioned that he was present when one of the spirits asked another, "Where is Ardiaeus the Great?" (Now this Ardiaeus lived a thousand years before the time of Er: he had been the tyrant of some city of Pamphylia, and had murdered his aged father and his elder brother, and was said to have committed many other abominable crimes.) The answer of the other spirit was: "He comes not hither and will never come. And this," said he, "was one of the dreadful sights which we ourselves witnessed. We were at the mouth of the cavern, and, having completed all our experiences, were about to reascend, when of a sudden Ardiaeus appeared and several others, most of whom were tyrants; and there were also besides the tyrants private individuals who had been great criminals: they were just, as they fancied, about to return into the upper world, but the mouth, instead of admitting them, gave a roar, whenever any of these incurable sinners or some one who had not been sufficiently punished tried to ascend; and then wild men of fiery aspect, who were standing by and heard the sound, seized and carried them off; and Ardiaeus and others they bound head and foot and hand, and threw them down and flayed them with scourges, and dragged them along the road at the side, carding them on thorns like wool, and declaring to the passers-by what were their crimes, and that they were being taken away to be cast into hell." And of all the many terrors, which they had endured, he said that there was none like the terror which each of them felt at that moment, lest they should hear the voice; and when there was silence, one by one they ascended with exceeding joy. These, said Er, were the penalties and retributions, and there were blessings as great.

"Now when the spirits which were in the meadow had tarried seven days, on the eighth they were obliged to proceed on their journey, and, on the fourth day after, he said that they came to a place where they could see from above a line of light, straight as a column, extending right through the whole heaven and through the earth, in color resembling the rainbow, only brighter and purer; another day's journey brought them to the place, and there, in the midst of the light, they saw the ends of the chains of heaven let down from above: for this light is the belt of heaven, and holds together the circle of the universe, like the under-girders of a trireme. From these ends is extended the spindle of Necessity, on which all the revolutions turn. The shaft and hook of this spindle are made of steel, and the whorl is made partly of steel and also partly of other materials. Now the whorl is in form like the whorl used on earth; and the description of it implied that there is one large hollow whorl which is quite scooped out, and into this is fitted another lesser one, and another, and another, and four others, making eight in all, like vessels which fit into one another; the whorls show their edges on the upper side, and on their lower side all together form one continuous whorl. This is pierced by the spindle, which is driven home through the centre of the eighth. The first and outermost whorl has the rim broadest, and the seven inner whorls are narrower, in the following proportions—the sixth is next to the first in size, the fourth next to the sixth; then comes the eighth; the seventh is fifth, the fifth is sixth, the third is seventh, last and eighth comes the second. The largest (of fixed stars) is spangled, and the seventh (or sun) is brightest; the eighth (or moon) colored by the reflected light of the seventh; the second and fifth (Saturn and Mercury) are in color like one another, and yellower than the preceding; the third (Venus) has the whitest light; the fourth (Mars) is reddish; the sixth (Jupiter) is in whiteness second. Now the whole spindle has the same motion; but, as the whole revolves in one direction, the seven inner circles move slowly in the other, and of these the swiftest is the eighth; next in swiftness are the seventh, sixth, and fifth, which move together; third in swiftness appeared to move according to the law of this reversed motion the fourth; the third appeared fourth and the second fifth. The spindle turns on the knees of Necessity; and on the upper surface of each circle is a siren, who goes round with them, hymning a single tone or note. The eight together form one harmony; and round about, at equal intervals, there is another band, three in number, each sitting upon her throne: these are the Fates, daughters of Necessity, who are clothed in white robes and have chaplets upon their heads, Lachesis and Clotho and Atropos, who accompany with their voices the harmony of the sirens—Lachesis singing of the past, Clotho of the present, Atropos of the future; Clotho from time to time assisting with a touch of her right hand the revolution of the outer circle of the whorl or spindle, and Atropos with her left hand touching and guiding the inner ones, and Lachesis laying hold of either in turn, first with one hand and then with the other.

"When Er and the spirits arrived, their duty was to go at once to Lachesis; but first of all there came a prophet who arranged them in order; then he took from the knees of Lachesis lots and samples of lives, and, having mounted a high pulpit, spoke as follows: "Hear the word of Lachesis, the daughter of Necessity. Mortal souls, behold a new cycle of life and mortality. Your genius will not be allotted to you, but you choose your genius; and let him who draws the first lot have the first choice, and the life which he chooses shall be his destiny. Virtue is free, and as a man honors or dishonors her he will have more or less of her; the responsibility is with the chooser— God is justified." When the Interpreter had thus spoken he scattered lots indifferently among them all, and each of them took up the lot which fell near him, all but Er himself (he was not allowed), and each as he took his lot perceived the number which he had obtained. Then the Interpreter placed on the ground before them the samples of lives; and there were many more lives than the souls present, and they were of all sorts. There were lives of every animal and of man in every condition. And there were tyrannies among them, some lasting out the tyrant's life, others which broke off in the middle and came to an end in poverty and exile and beggary; and there were lives of famous men, some who were famous for their form and beauty as well as for their strength and success in games, or, again, for their birth and the qualities of their ancestors; and some who were the reverse of famous for the opposite qualities. And of women likewise; there was not, however, any definite character to them, because the soul, when choosing a new life, must of necessity become different. But there was every other quality, and the all mingled with one another, and also with elements of wealth and poverty, and disease and health; and there were mean states also. And here, my dear Glaucon, is the supreme peril of our human state, and therefore the utmost care should be taken. Let each one of us leave every other kind of knowledge and seek and follow one thing only, if peradventure he may be able to learn and may find some one who will make him able to learn and discern between good and evil, and so to choose always and everywhere the better life as he has opportunity. He should consider the bearing of all these things which have been mentioned severally and collectively upon virtue; he should know what the effect of beauty is when combined with poverty or wealth in a particular soul, and what are the good and evil consequences of noble and humble birth, of private and public station, of strength and weakness, of cleverness and dullness, and of all the soul, and the operation of them when conjoined; he will then look at the nature of the soul, and from the consideration of all these qualities he will be able to determine which is the better and which is the worse; and so he will choose, giving the name of evil to the life which will make his soul more unjust, and good to the life which will make his soul more just; all else he will disregard. For we have seen and know that this is the best choice both in life and after death. A man must take with him into the world below an adamantine faith in truth and right, that there, too, he may be undazzled by the desire of wealth or the other allurements of evil, lest, coming upon tyrannies and similar villainies, he do irremediable wrongs to others and suffer yet worse himself; but let him know how to choose the mean and avoid the extremes on either side, as far as possible, not only in this life but in all that which is to come. For this is the way of happiness.

"And according to the report of the messenger from the other world this was what the prophet said at the time: "Even for the last comer, if he chooses wisely and will live diligently, there is appointed a happy and not undesirable existence. Let not him who chooses first be careless, and let not the last despair." And when he had spoken, he who had the first choice came forward and, in a moment, chose the greatest tyranny; his mind having been darkened by folly and sensuality, he had not thought out the whole matter before he chose, and did not at first sight perceive that he was fated, among other evils, to devour his own children. But when he had time to reflect, and saw what was in the lot, he began to beat his breast and lament over his choice, forgetting the proclamation of the prophet; for, instead of throwing the blame of his misfortune on himself, he accused chance and the gods, and everything rather than himself. Now he was one of those who came from heaven, and in a former life had dwelt in a well-ordered State, but his virtue was a matter of habit only, and he had no philosophy. And it was true of others who were similarly overtaken, that the greater number of them came from heaven and therefore they had never been schooled by trial, whereas the pilgrims who came from earth, having themselves suffered and seen others suffer, were not in a hurry to choose. And owing to this inexperience of theirs, and also because the lot was a chance, many of the souls exchanged a good destiny for an evil or an evil for a good. For if a man had always on his arrival in this world dedicated himself from the first to sound philosophy, and had been moderately fortunate in the number of the lot, he might, as the messenger reported, be happy here, and also his journey to another life and return to this, instead of being rough and underground, would be smooth and heavenly. Most curious, he said, was the spectacle—sad and laughable and strange; for the choice of the souls was, in most cases, based on their experience of a previous life. There he saw the soul which had once been Orpheus choosing the life of a swan out of enmity to the race of women, hating to be born of a woman because they had been his murderers; he beheld also the soul of Thamyras choosing the life of a nightingale; birds, on the other hand, like the swan and other musicians, wanting to be men. The soul which obtained the twentieth lot chose the life of a lion, and this was the soul of Ajax the son of Telamon, who would not be a man, remembering the injustice which was done him the judgment about the arms. The next was Agamemnon, who took the life of an eagle, because, like Ajax, he hated human nature by reason of his sufferings. About the middle came the lot of Atalanta; she, seeing the great fame of an athlete, was unable to resist the temptation: and after her there followed the soul of Epeus the son of Panopeus passing into the nature of a woman cunning in the arts; and far away among the last who chose, the soul of the jester Thersites was putting on the form of a monkey. There came also the soul of Odysseus having yet to make a choice, and his lot happened to be the last of them all. Now the recollection of former toils had disenchanted him of ambition, and he went about for a considerable time in search of the life of a private man who had no cares; he had some difficulty in finding this, which was lying about and had been neglected by everybody else; and when he saw it, he said that he would have done the same had his lot been first instead of last, and that he was delighted to have it. And not only did men pass into animals, but I must also mention that there were animals tame and wild who changed into one another and into corresponding human natures—the good into the gentle and the evil into the savage, in all sorts of combinations.

"All the souls had now chosen their lives, and they went in the order of their choice to Lachesis, who sent with them the genius whom they had severally chosen, to be the guardian of their lives and the fulfiller of the choice: this genius led the souls first to Clotho, and drew them within the revolution of the spindle impelled by her hand, thus ratifying the destiny of each; and then, when they were fastened to this, carried them to Atropos, who spun the threads and made them irreversible, whence without turning round they passed beneath the throne of Necessity; and when they had all passed, they marched on in a scorching heat to the plain of Forgetfulness, which was a barren waste destitute of trees and verdure; and then towards evening they encamped by the river of Unmindfulness, whose water no vessel can hold; of this they were all obliged to drink a certain quantity, and those who were not saved by wisdom drank more than was necessary; and each one as he drank forgot all things. Now after they had gone to rest, about the middle of the night there was a thunderstorm and earthquake, and then in an instant they were driven upwards in all manner of ways to their birth, like stars shooting. He himself was hindered from drinking the water. But in what manner or by what means he returned to the body he could not say; only, in the morning, awaking suddenly, he found himself lying on the pyre.

"And thus, Glaucon, the tale has been saved and has not perished, and will save us if we are obedient to the word spoken; and we shall pass safely over the river of Forgetfulness and our soul will not be defiled. Wherefore my counsel is that we hold fast ever to the heavenly way and follow after justice and virtue always, considering that the soul is immortal and able to endure every sort of good and every sort of evil. Thus shall we live dear to one another and to the gods, both while remaining here and when, like conquerors in the games, who go round to gather gifts, we receive our reward. And it shall be well with us both in this life and in the pilgrimage of a thousand years which we have been describing."

∼

It's interesting that even in Plato's time they thought Er's experience was more than just a dream because it wouldn't have been unreasonable to conclude it was just that. In the case of modern day NDEs and STEs (which in effect appear to be the same thing), what separates them from a normal dream is, (1) due to the person's physiological state, doctors know the patient wouldn't be physically capable of dreaming, (2) the experiencer sometimes sees what's going on in the local environment, such as the operating theater, from an elevated out-of-body point of view, (3) experiencers meet deceased people they had no way of knowing had died before their NDE, and (4) the life changing after-effects it has on the experiencer.

None of this is *proof* of survival (because there is no such thing as proof) but it does demonstrate that something appears to be going on that can't be explained by the five senses.

In the twenty-first century these experiences are more commonplace than ever before, in part, because resuscitation techniques such as the use of defibrillators are keeping people alive who, in the past, would have succumbed to their injuries and illnesses. But in the 1700s, a near-death experience was probably rare, and rarer still was someone who shared their experience with others and documented it.

Even today, many people keep these experiences to themselves for fear of being mocked, but the tide is turning and the Internet is linking people all over the world who have had an experience and others who want to know more about them.

In the case below, a seaman participating in The Seven Years' War was close to death and had an NDE where he met an acquaintance who he later discovered had died. I can understand why having the knowledge that an acquaintance had died, something he didn't know prior to the NDE, had a profound effect on him for the next thirty years until he finally told his story.

Recollections of an old Soldier

It is late autumn, 1762 ...

"While I was on board that vessel, it appears to me that I died, that I went through the excruciating pains of the separating of soul and body, as completely as ever I shall again, (and such a separation must soon take place) and that I was immediately conveyed to the gate of heaven, and was going to pass in, but was told by one, that I could not enter then, but in process of time, if I would behave as he directed, on the set time I should have admittance. It appeared to me that my feet stood on a firm foundation, and that I stood there for the space of about a half hour. In this time there appeared to be a continual flowing up of people, as we suppose they die, and none stopped, but all passed off one way or the other. Just at my left hand, there appeared to be the opening of a great gulf, and the greater part of the grown people seemed to pass off there.

"Once in a while one passed through the gate into the Holy City. One person appeared, with whom I had been intimately acquainted, and it appeared to me that I knew him as well as ever I did: it was Dr. Matthews (and whether I saw him or not, he died, as I afterwards learned, while I was sick on board the ship).

"The one that talked with me, told me about the Revolutionary War, and showed me the British vessels in the harbor of Boston, as plainly as I saw them when they came. And, during the first year of that war, I was down there in Gen. Putnam's regiment, and I went on Roxbury hill to see the shipping in the harbor, and they looked exactly as they had been shown to me many years before. This transition (as I firmly believe) from life to death, and from death to life, which took place nearly sixty years ago, is as fresh in my mind now as it was then, and not many days have passed from that time to this, which have not brought the interesting scenes I then witnessed, clearly to view in my mind. But I never dared to say any thing about it, for a great many years afterwards, for fear of being ridiculed.

"About the [last of February or first of January, 1763], peace was declared between England, France and Spain, and the people rejoiced exceedingly on account of it. I told them we should have another war soon. They asked me why I thought so. I told them the British had settled peace with their foreign enemies, but they could not long live in peace, and they would come against us next.

"I never told my own wife, nor any other person, of what happened to me on board the vessel, as above related, for nearly thirty years afterwards, when a great deal was said in the neighborhood where I lived, about one Polly Davis of Grantham, N.H., who was taken very sick, so that no one thought she could live long, and many times the people thought she was dying. In one of these turns she had a dream or vision, by which she was assured that, on a stated Sunday, she should be healed, and [should] go to [the] meeting the same day. On the Saturday night, previous to the time appointed, many people stood round her bed, expecting every moment that she would breathe her last: but when the hour she had mentioned arrived, she rose from her bed, and said she was well: and Captain Robert Scott carried her some distance to the meeting, behind him on horseback, the same day she recovered. There was so much talk about it, that I ventured to tell my experience as before described, and have since told it to a great many people; and some believe it, and others do not."[27]

Bathed in the Light

In 1969 Bill Vandenbush, like many young Americans, went to fight in the Vietnam War. During his first year he witnessed the horrors of that war—the trauma, carnage, and the death of friends and comrades.

One day, while out on patrol, his squad came under attack; "My squad got pinned down," he wrote in his book, *If Morning Never Comes*.[28] "In a few minutes the gunshots started coming at us from all directions. It was heavier than ever. I knew it was more than just Viet Cong snipers or an NVA squad; it seemed more like a fully armed NVA Company. We continued taking heavy fire and I got down in a shallow trench."

Bill called for an airstrike and, as the plane dropped its first load, he realized they had dropped the bombs too early and that on their second run he would be in the kill zone.

He writes; "Just before the bombs landed I took a quick peek to see how close they were going to hit. I saw the bright flash, but before I could get my head back down a big piece of red-hot shrapnel hit me in the face. The searing pain jolted my head back and my steel helmet tumbled to the ground. Smaller pieces of razor sharp shrapnel hit me in the neck and down the right side of my body. There was no denial; I knew immediately that I was very seriously injured. The right side of my face was crushed by the baseball-sized piece of shrapnel from the bomb. The blood gushed from the wound and pooled beneath me in the dirt. I leaned forward to pick up my steel helmet and, to my horror, I watched what was left of my right eye fall out into the helmet."

Bill lay down in the fetal position and accepted he was about to die. It was then that he had an experience that would change his life.

"I still had a slight sensation of belonging to my body," he explains. "I was still wounded, but there was no bleeding and no pain. I felt no fear, worry or concern as the darkness enveloped me. I was walking, no, not walking, gliding forward effortlessly at an incline, propelled by an unknown force.

"I was inside a dark tunnel ... and I had no sense of anything solid in any direction. It was completely dark all around me yet I seemed to be aglow with a dim light that emanated from within my heart. I was bathed in this soft light as I continued to glide forward. As the light washed over me, I felt an incredible sense of calm. ..."

"Suddenly, I was thrust from the darkness into a bright white light. The White Light surrounded me and at the same time I was one with the Light. ... I no longer possessed my body. I was now a being consisting entirely of Light and Energy. ..."

"This place was filled with love, beautiful unconditional love. ... I had no worry, no fear, no stress, no pressure, and no concern about anything. ..."

"The memory of my entire nineteen-year-old life was slowly fading, diminishing and being replaced by a great sense of universal oneness. I was a ball of Energy... Light Energy. I was in a different dimension of existence than I had been on earth. ..."

"I had only the slightest recollection of what had just happened to me on the battlefield, however, my personality and the essence of my worldly existence was still intact. ..."

"At one point, I was approached by another ball of Light Energy that began to communicate with me. It wasn't a verbal conversation; it was more like a telepathic exchange, an understanding of what was being communicated without using words or voice. I recognized this Light Being as my grandfather, the one who taught me to drink whiskey and smoke cigars, who had died several years before. He told me "Everything is wonderful here. Allow yourself to be one with the Light."

"Everything is even more beautiful beyond this point and when you get there you will be able to explore the entire universe."

Bill continues, "We talked for a short time about having faith and trusting the Light. He reassured me, saying: 'Things are going to be fine, but you must have faith no matter what happens.' I was beginning to see beyond this place of Light. ..."

"While I was conversing with my grandfather and having more heavenly visions, a third ball of energy, a strong Spirit Being, but not one entirely familiar to me, came toward us. My grandfather said: 'This is Great Spirit; he is not the only Great Spirit, but he is one of the eldest and most evolved of Spirits.' Great Spirit told me in a stern but kind voice: "You can't stay here. You must return to your earthly place. When you have fulfilled your higher purpose you will again come to the Light. ..."

"Great Spirit is not a religious being; He is a Spirit of all things living; A Spirit of the Universe, and of all people, places and things throughout the Universe. It became clear to me that all living things are connected by Spirit and that Spirit lives within us, and within all living things.

"Finally, like a good soldier, I obeyed and turned. I was suddenly back in the dark tunnel. I was gliding back in the opposite direction from which I had originally come. My body was full of White Light and glowing brightly. I had a strength that I had never felt before. Suddenly, I snapped back into my body. Oddly though, there was no pain. I was still critically injured and bleeding, but I felt no pain. I was at peace and everything seemed clearer and more in focus. I had moved through the dark corridor and I was back in Vietnam."

That event was to be Bill's "Road to Damascus" moment: a "before and after" event that changed his life forever. Like many experiencers he found himself detached from his physical body and in a tunnel. He met his "dead" grandfather who shared the wisdom that he had gleaned since he had crossed the threshold. He met a beautiful being—The Great Spirit, who assured Bill that it wasn't his time.

Like the seaman in the Seven Years War, the recollection has stayed with him. I had a Skype conversation with Bill forty-five years after his "conversion" and he said that what he experienced was still as clear to him as the day it happened. His experience has enabled him to deal with his injuries and overcome them with grace and gratitude, and in turn helped him to help others who are struggling with the trials of life.

Speaking of roads to Damascus, what are we to think about one of the most famous spiritual conversions in history? I'm referring to St Paul in the Bible.

In 2 Corinthians 12:2[29] Paul the Apostle a.k.a. Saul of Tarsus wrote:

> I know a man in Christ who, fourteen years ago, was caught up to the third heaven. Whether it was in the body or out of it I do not know, but God knows. And I know that this man—whether in the body or out of it I do not know, but God knows—was caught up into Paradise. The things he heard were too sacred for words, things that man is not permitted to tell.

The third heaven, or the Persian word, "paradise" meaning the "walled garden," both sound remarkably similar to the "third sphere" and the "garden," which communicators "in spirit" repeatedly refer to as the dimension that many humans find themselves in after physical death. Was Paul having to a near-death experience or an out-of-body experience?

Likewise, Paul's "Road to Damascus."

In Acts 9:1-30,[30] while on the road …

> … he neared Damascus on his journey, suddenly a light from heaven flashed around him. He fell to the ground and heard a voice say to him, "Saul, Saul, why do you persecute me?"
>
> "Who are you, Lord?" Saul asked.
>
> "I am Jesus, whom you are persecuting," he replied. "Now get up and go into the city, and you will be told what you must do."
>
> The men traveling with Saul stood there speechless; they heard the sound but did not see anyone. Saul got up from the ground, but when he opened his eyes he could see nothing. So they led him by the hand into Damascus. For three days he was blind, and did not eat or drink anything.

There are differences of opinion of what actually happened to Paul and whether his followers heard the voice or he alone, but assuming the event actually took place, it's clear that it was a spiritually transformative experience, which was life-changing for him.

Two thousand years later, some skeptics, psychiatrists and physicians have suggested that Paul suffered from sunstroke or had a seizure or a mood disorder, and, of course in theory, severe sunstroke or a seizure could be life-threatening and trigger an event such as an NDE. But that doesn't take anything away from the effect it had on him and a good percentage of the world's population ever since.

It is thought that his conversion happened when he was around thirty-years old and that he was executed when he was around sixty-years old, and, during the thirty years between his conversion and his death, he wrote thirteen of the letters in the New Testament (although some are disputed) which, in turn, helped to shape the world as we know it today. That's quite something for a man with a bad case of sunstroke.

Heaven never helps the man who will not act.

~ SOPHOCLES

4
PRESIDENT ROOSEVELT'S SECRETARY COMMUNICATES FROM THE AFTERLIFE

Charles Fryer

During the first half of the twentieth century, Geraldine Cummins (1890-1969) was Ireland's most celebrated psychic. As with Tudor-Pole in chapter 1, her particular mediumship manifested as "automatic writing" where, allegedly, controlled by discarnate beings, the medium is able to write, sometimes with authority, on matters normally outside his or her own knowledge.

Cummins was never found to be anything less than genuine and, at times, even she was skeptical of the material she received psychically. Nevertheless, she produced impressive evidence that our consciousness survives physical death; evidence, furthermore, that was considered bona fide by the majority of the recipients despite her own skepticism.

The author of this chapter, Charles Fryer, was a schoolmaster and college lecturer who was ordained in 1963 at the age of forty-nine, but, apart from a three-years curacy in Coventry, he remained in full-time education as a lecturer in history until his retirement.

He later became priest-in-charge to two small Episcopal congregations in the Scottish Highlands, and a part-time tutor in Liturgical Studies for the Geneva Theological College.

Fryer became interested in parapsychology in 1968 after reading an article in the Christian journal, "Modern Churchman" by John Pearce-Higgins. The article was on the subject of psychical research and its relevance to the Christian doctrine of immortality. Three years later Fryer discovered he also had the gift of automatic writing, which prompted him to investigate Geraldine Cummins in detail.

The communication, below, took place in 1945. Geraldine Cummins was the medium and Miss Gibbes, the sitter. Geraldine's Control was called Astor. Geraldine didn't like the term, "control" and she wrote in her book, *Swan on a Black Sea*: "I dislike the word "control," commonly used in psychic research for the guardian caretaker of a medium. Mine, Astor, has never controlled me. I prefer that long gone medium Socrates's own name for his subliminal caretaker, which was "Daimon."

During this sitting a communicator claiming to be Marguerite Le Hand, who had died a year earlier in

PRESIDENT ROOSEVELT'S SECRETARY COMMUNICATES

1944, came through trying to get a message to David Gray, the US minister for Ireland. Gray was known to Geraldine and, in life, Marguerite had been private secretary to Franklin D. Roosevelt, the then U.S. President.

～

The scripts so far considered in this book[31] were either ostensibly from persons in the remote past, evidence for whose historical existence could not be forthcoming, or from persons who, though Geraldine had not known them personally, had made names for themselves in one way or another, so that she might have gained knowledge about them through reading or hearing about them, before forgetting that she had done so. It is less easy to disparage or explain away the two sequences with which the present chapter deals, since, when the first contacts were made, she had never heard of either person.

The first appeared as a "drop-in communicator," during a session when some of Miss Gibbes' discarnate relatives were communicating, and asked to be put into touch with a named person, validating her existence by giving some pieces of information which turned out later to be quite correct and which, if genuine discarnate contact be set aside as impossible, could be explained only if Geraldine's mind possessed an astonishing degree of super-ESP, ranging widely into the minds of people whom she had never met as well as some she knew, selecting pieces of mental material and combining them into a coherent whole in a manner for which no precedent exists. If this incredible ability may be supposed to exist, why boggle at survival?

At the time when these communications were received she was in a poor state of health. She had just returned from a long period of wartime residence in southern Ireland where she had been nursing her mother until the latter's death late in 1944. Despite her indisposition she made a few attempts to write automatically for her friend's benefit, and, during a session on March 19th 1945, the following passage appeared in what her control Astor was saying:

"I must tell you there is a stranger here, a quiet gray-haired woman with a curious force ... She says she died in Chelsea. She shows me a hand, that is her surname, I gather. Then a daisy. Yes, Marguerite Le Hand. She says she worked for a long time with an important public man—knew him well. She gives the name Frank. She says she wants to talk to David about Frank, and that David hopes to come to this town [presumably London] in April. If so, she begs that you see him for the writing, not to let anything interfere as she has something important to say about Frank ... You may know in April, as David is likely to want to see you if he has time. . . . That is all about her now. She doesn't seem able to give surnames. She seems to have been over here about three years. She says her message is important in regard to future peace."

Geraldine herself, as was usually the case, was unaware of what she had written. Miss Gibbes, putting the name "Frank" and the designation "important public man" together, guessed that the American President Roosevelt was being referred to.

When the session was over, Geraldine said she remembered something about David Gray; this latter was the United States Minister in Dublin, whom she had met more than once when she was in Ireland and who was interested in her psychic abilities; he also happened to be related to Roosevelt. So, immediately after the communication, they had some inkling of what the message might be about but none on the actual identity of the communicator. The statement that the latter had died in Chelsea misled Miss Gibbes, who naturally assumed that Chelsea, London, was meant, since she lived there herself, and she tried to trace locally the death of someone named Le Hand, but without success. However, her curiosity had been aroused and, at a session six days later, she made a point of asking for "the quiet gray-haired stranger you described the other day." Further information was now forthcoming.

"She was an interesting woman with a keen brain, extremely quick but quiet, like one who had very great self-control and grip of herself. ... She knows David Gray. ..." When I asked her who Frank was she replied that he was a man of affairs, and did not seem to wish to give more information. I said, was he in business, and she replied that he was the most important businessman in his country. ... She seems to have had a confidential post with Frank. ... David would know her. ... She did not particularly wish that you should find out who she was. ... That was her habit in life, to keep secrets, and so she was always reserved with strangers. [Miss Gibbes then remarked that she had not been able to find any reference to her having died in Chelsea.] She said, "There is more than one Chelsea in the world," and smiled.

The third communication from the gray-haired woman was, like the first one, apparently initiated by herself. She gave her name, Marguerite Le Hand, directly without recourse to symbolic imagery, said she had originally communicated because she wanted to warn David Gray that "Frank was coming over," corrected Miss Gibbes' misapprehension by saying she had died in Chelsea, Massachusetts, commented on her successor's abilities— "Ann is very clever but hasn't the experience," said again that she had worked for "Frank" in a confidential position, and that "Frank" was now resting, "after the passage of death." This was on April 14th 1945, two days after President Roosevelt's sudden death, which was, of course, generally known in Britain almost as soon as it happened.

It was now time to contact David Gray, and natural that Geraldine should undertake this task since he and she were already acquainted. She wrote him a letter expressing her sympathy for him at the President's death, and added a note to the effect that a Marguerite Le Hand had "called in March and was worried about something happening to a friend of his in April. She said she was from Chelsea, Mass." It was necessary to write vaguely since correspondence was still being censored if sent to Southern Ireland, but she believed that Gray would be able to put two and two together, which he did. He replied confirming that Roosevelt had indeed had a secretary named Marguerite Le Hand, and that this lady had died about two years earlier in Chelsea, Massachusetts, and that, though relatively young, she had had white hair.

He asked if he might be sent excerpts from the scripts.

Beatrice Gibbes answered the letter, not by sending excerpts but by asking eight specific questions about matters mentioned in the scripts. To each of these he replied affirmatively and added three questions of his own, to be posed the next time she was contacted in a session.

At a fourth session these questions were put. The communicator seemed to wish to avoid answering two of them, which were about herself, but, in response to the third, correctly gave the name of her successor as secretary to the President, the highly unusual surname of Boettiger. She also mentioned a friend of the President who had predeceased him, giving his first name and the initial of his surname correctly. Gray was notified the results of the session and, in reply, confirmed the correctness of what was said and expressed special surprise at the mention of 'Edwin W.' (He was actually General Watson, who had died suddenly on the ship which brought the President and his entourage back from the Crimea after the Yalta Conference in mid-February 1945.)

At the fifth session, on June 6th, further attempts to probe were made, but the communicator now appeared to become cautious and suspicious. However, she did give one remarkable piece of information: she communicated her second name, which few people knew and David Gray did not know. This was Alice.

Geraldine returned to Ireland for a summer holiday soon afterwards, and, on June 20, had a session at writing with Gray and his wife at their Dublin home. This time Roosevelt himself appeared to come through, and, beside the expected personal remarks, added some trivial information of the sort that sitters often find singularly convincing.

"I well remember that last warm morning. I think it was horror at the prospect of a detestable lunch of gruel that made me collapse ... I was very active at my funeral, and the only one who paid attention to me was Scottie, my dog ... When my dog saw me he rolled on the ground, making quite a bit of diversion. But nobody guessed he rolled on the grass with joy because he saw me."

It had been a nice morning, the President had had gruel just before his lunch (a food which indeed he did not relish) and the dog was a Scottish terrier who was in the habit of rolling over when meeting someone he liked.

It was not possible to continue this intriguing investigation since Geraldine had to go into hospital for a serious operation, which was followed by a long period of convalescence. The case was reported in the *Journal of the Society of Psychical Research* for May 1947, with assumed names being substituted for the real ones. Enough facts had certainly been correctly conveyed, facts all of which were unknown to Geraldine and Beatrice Gibbes and some also to David Gray, to make it almost impossible to suppose that their production was the consequence of chance guesswork.

One may surely also rule out the suggestion of a conspiracy to deceive the world (or that small part of the world which is interested in psychic disclosures) on the parts of those three persons. Had ESP between living persons not been established as a fact, the likelihood of there having been discarnate contact would have been overwhelmingly great.

As it is, if it were a telepathic tour de force it involved astonishing psychic virtuosity. Is it really believable that a middle-aged woman of moderate educational attainments (though considerable intelligence) who was in a poor state of health, with a cancer which needed removing, had the mental agility to reach out at incredible speed across the oceans, and select, from the memories of people she had never heard, of facts which could be processed in her own mind and then emerge as convincing little dramatic episodes. How could she have known about the President's gruel? How could she have become aware of the surname Boettiger? Did she fish or was she told? The former seems as unlikely as sitting with a rod at the end of Brighton pier and catching a fish, which one particular person several thousand miles away had marked beforehand.

Almost as strange as the disclosure of evidential detail is the way in which the communicator, who had deliberately taken the initiative in the first and third sessions, became cautious and wary in the fifth. This was quite in keeping with her character as the secretary of an important political person. If Geraldine had been fishing for clues with her wide-ranging mind, one would have supposed she might have found some, to make her impersonation stronger.

The fool thinks, "I am the body," the intelligent man thinks, "I am an individual soul united with the body." But the wise man, in the greatness of his knowledge and spiritual discrimination, sees the Self as the only reality and thinks, "I am Brahman."

~ ADI SHANKARA

5
RESCUE CIRCLES

Lord Dowding

As mentioned in chapter 2, Lord Dowding regularly attended or hosted a "rescue circle where one or more mediums sit with a small group of sitters—the aim being to reach people who have died and are confused about their situation or have no idea they are dead. During World War II, with the number of people dying en masse, this must have been common.

In *God's Magic*, explaining the method of "rescue" Dowding wrote: "Awakening work was the commonest type during the war, when casualties were heavy and when the crowds in the astral were continually being reinforced by fresh contingents of men suddenly wiped out of earthly existence and quite unaware of what had happened to them.

"What generally used to occur was that we would be sitting in the drawing room of the lady who acted as medium and whom I have designated L. L. for the purpose of these records. All the surroundings would be quite normal in ordinary or artificial light according to the time of year. Then L. L. perhaps would say: 'Here are three paratroopers from Normandy' or 'Here is the crew of a bomber who think that they have come down in the Ruhr,' or something like that, and then we would hold them in quiet conversation while those on the other side were working on them to raise their vibrations: and after a bit they would begin to notice something strange in our appearance, something different from themselves, or, by trying to shake hands or to slap me on the back they would discover that we were intangible and the little shock of the discovery would bring realization, but somehow or other they always eventually tumbled to what had happened, and then they could see the friends who had come to meet them and they would all go off happily together.

I have reproduced three of these cases here."

We had just finished our healing circle when Chang (a Chinese guide) told us that he had someone for us to awaken.

L. L. "It is an American flying boy; he can't see us or anything yet. Will you conduct the conversation? I shall be too far away." (From this point L. L. was in a semi-trance. She spoke with a strong American accent and her face worked in accordance with the emotions of the boy.)

Boy. "Say, what's this? Where am I?"

Self. "It's all right. You have been brought to us so that we may help you."

Boy. "Oh, never mind about me! Help the others—help the others. I've just seen one of them have his leg snapped off by a croc."

Self. "It's all right. The others are being helped."

(But he was difficult to pacify. He wanted me to go and help them.)

"Can you see me now?"

Boy. "Sure, I can see you. But you keep on acting funny; kinda shimmering like a bad movie."

Self. "Yes. I want you to look closely at us and you will see that we do not look solid and real to you. And when you can see that we are not real, then you will be able to see the others who have come to help you."

Boy. "Say, where am I?"

Self. "You are in England."

Boy. "Well, that's a good one! We were flying over. … No, I mustn't tell you; but one of those Japs got us and we couldn't stay in the air."

Self. "You came down out of control?"

Boy. "We were on fire. But we all got out except Tubby. Tubby was in the tail. A damned death trap that is! Sorry I can't tell you where we were flying."

Self. "Never mind about the Official Secrets Act now; it doesn't affect you any more. I tell you again that this is England—just near London."

Boy. "Say, I've always wanted to visit England, but I never thought it would be like this. But who are you, anyway?"

Self. "You've been brought to me so that I may help you."

Boy. "Yes, but who are you?"

Self. "Well, you've heard of the Battle of Britain. Did you ever hear of Sir Hugh Dowding?"

Boy. "Why, yes; sure I've heard of him. I know old Dowding."

Self. "Well, I'm old Dowding. I really am. Come on now, put your hand on my shoulder."

Boy. "How can I put my hand on your shoulder when you keep jumping about?" (Of course I hadn't moved.)

Self. "All right, then, smack me on the back. A good hard one." Boy (tries it and encounters no resistance). "Gosh! Are you a ghost?"

Self. "No, I'm not a ghost."

Boy. "Am I a ghost, then?"

Self. "No. What has happened is that you and I are in different worlds."

Boy. "How do you mean, different worlds? You just said we were both here in England. (Suddenly he realizes, and his face puckers up into an expression of agony.) "Why, I haven't been all that bad; I don't have to go to hell!"

Self. "No, no, no. You aren't going to hell. We're just trying to wake you up so that you can go and join all your friends."—A pause.

Boy. (with a sudden flood of delight). "Why, MAC. How in hell did you get here? (To me). I'll be okay now. Mac's a great guy. Mac taught me to fly."

Another long pause, then ...

Boy. (his face lighting up with indescribable awe, reverence and joy. Speaking very slowly). "Today shalt thou be with Me in Paradise. Well, I'm no worse than the thief, and I guess I will be. (He talks to Mac for a little, then —) Say, I understand now. Mac got his too. (Sees Tubby.) Why, Tubby, how did you get here?"

Tubby. (apparently so called because he is very tall and extremely thin). "We're all here. We've been here all the time, but we couldn't see one another nor see you; we could only hear your voice." (Now they can all see one another and are talking together.)

After the healing circle on March 30th, 1944, James (deceased, who commanded a squadron in the Battle of Britain) said: "We have a crew for you to wake up. It shouldn't be a difficult job. My heart is very much in this because some of my friends are among them. They are not here yet: as a matter of fact they are walking along the road outside. They will come in here."

L. L. "Here they are, seven of them. The leader seems to be a squadron leader with fair, wavy hair. Now they are looking at a big picture on the wall. They can't see us yet. They think they are in Germany. One of them says: 'They seem to be quite civilised people here. I mean to say, this is a very nicely furnished and home-like room.' "They move over to the piano. One of them wishes to play. I say, 'You won't be able to open it,' and I go across and open the piano.'

L. L. "He didn't like that! He says, 'Gosh, this house must be haunted.'" She describes some other members of the crew, a ginger haired lad and a little dark Jewish-looking boy.

L .L. "Now they are beginning to see us. They can't understand the new dimensions." With ten people in it the room ought to be crowded, but it doesn't seem to be. Five of them are sitting on the music seat, meant to accommodate two. Now the leader begins to talk to me. He says, 'How is it that you are talking English?'

Self. "Because I am English."

Leader. "Where are we, then?"

Self. "This is Wimbledon; do you know it?"

Leader. "I should just say I do!"

Self. "All right, then. You have just been walking along the Worple Road."

Leader. "But how did we get here? We must have come down over the Ruhr."

Self. "You have been brought here that we may help you."

Leader. "But who are you?"

I go to the mantelpiece, take down a picture of myself in uniform, and hold it beside my face.

Self. "Do you know who I am now?" Yes. They all recognise me now. One says, "I remember you when you came to inspect us at Biggin Hill."

Leader. "How can you help us?"

Self. "Oh, just by talking to you and helping you to realize your position. Do you see me clearly? Do I look natural?"

Leader. "Yes, of course you do."

Self. "Very well, then. Shake hands." (I hold out my hand.)

Leader. "I can't get hold of it. Why don't you grip my hand?"

Self. "All right, I will. Watch very carefully" (and I slowly close my hand through his without his feeling anything).

L. L. "He didn't like that!" Just then the dark lad comes up behind and gives me a terrific smack on the back. He utters a shrill Cockney yelp as his hand encounters no resistance.

Leader. "Look here, Sir, are you trying to tell us that we are—that this is death?"

Self. "Yes. That is exactly what I have been trying to get you to realize."

Leader. "But how can we be dead? We are just as we were before."

Self. "Yes. Now you can see what a ridiculous little barrier death is. This death, which everyone is so frightened of. (Now he can see James. I introduce them.) Talk to him and he will be able to explain much more than I can." The tail gunner says: "I remember a Hun fighter coming up behind and knowing that something was going to happen. Then I remember no more until we were in the road outside." James explains that they were all blown to pieces instantaneously in their aeroplane three or four days previously over the Ruhr.

Now they can see all their other R.A.F. friends who have come to meet them and they all go off together.

May 22nd, 1944.

L. L. "Here are two R.A.F. boys wearing 'Mae West ' jackets. One has hurt his ankle and is nursing it.

He is very dark, with a black moustache. The other, very fair, is smoking a cigarette. The dark one is cursing freely: his companion says: 'Stow it. Come on. Lean on me.

Hop a bit and see where we can get to.' Here are two more coming along. One is a tiny Cockney."

The Fair One. "Where is Galbraith?"

The Tiny One. "We can't find him."

The Fair One. "The deuce we can't. He is the only one likely to know where we are."

The Tiny One. "I think I know where we are. I think we are in Germany. Look, the river isn't far away; but we can't have been over here very much, there's not enough damage." Now the fair one has seen us.

The Fair One. "I don't understand this. One moment we are out of doors and the next we are in a house."

The Dark One. "I don't care. Here's a chair." (Sits down.) They can all see us now.

The Tiny One. "Wait a minute. I'll try and find out what the old chap's writing."

Self. "Yes. Come and have a look over my shoulder."

The Fair One. "Just a moment. You are speaking English. Can you tell us where we are?"

Self. "You are in Wimbledon."

The Fair One. "Will you help us to get back?"

Self. "Where do you want to go?" (But they won't tell me, for security reasons.)

Self. "As a matter of fact I know where you want to go."

The Fair One. "It's strange, but I don't want to move." They go on asking after Galbraith, who was their navigator. I ask L. L. "Is James there? James, what happened to Galbraith?"

James. "Galbraith baled out." (I tell them this.)

The Tiny One. "That's a good joke! What should he want to bale out for? Nothing happened to us. We're all right." James explains that the machine blew up. It was blown into halves. Galbraith was able to escape by parachute.

They overhear but don't understand.

Self. "Galbraith got away with it, but you four didn't."

The Fair One. "What do you mean? We're here all right."

Self. (to Tiny). " Give me a smack on the back, will you?"

The Tiny One. "Watch me!" (Tries.) "Oh! So you're made of India rubber, are you?" (Tries again.)

The Fair One. "Stop it now! Yes, thanks, I see."

The Tiny One. (dancing about). "We're spooks, we're spooks, we're spooks!"

They begin to see us looking shimmery and unreal. I tell them to look round and I tell them who James is.

They see him.

The Fair One. (saluting James). "Reporting for duty, Sir." Now they see all the great crowd of the Boys.

The fair one can't see me any more, but thanks us nicely.

He says: "There's nothing to worry about. We're exactly as we were."

The Tiny One. "If we're spooks, Tyndall's leg isn't broken, is it?"

Self. "No. He will find he can use it if he tries."

The Tiny One. "Go on, then. Get up, you lazy lump!"

The Dark One. (recognising a friend). "Why, hello, Bill! You see we couldn't let you fellows steal a march on us. We've caught up—we've caught up!"

Now, I shouldn't like anyone to get the idea this is the only way in which these lads are awakened to their new life, or that we are the only operators of this particular method.

Quite a number of people are engaged in this work, but for some reason or other, it is very little known. Also you must remember that every little drama, such as I have described, is watched by numbers of unseen spectators who see what is happening and apply the illumination to their own conditions.

At the time when our circle was in full activity it was, perhaps, natural that most of those brought to us for help should have been war casualties, and that among them airmen should preponderate. But of course there were tens, and perhaps hundreds of thousands of civilian war casualties in this country alone, and when we add to these the casualties from the bombing of Germany and Japan and other countries, both allied and enemy, it will readily be imagined what a tremendous task lay (and lies) before the celestial 'rescue squads' in coping with this vast drifting population of bemused and earthbound souls.

Of course I do not, for a moment, suggest that everyone who was killed by a bomb became earthbound; but it is no use shutting our eyes to unpleasant facts, and it is an unpleasant fact that a great number of such people do become earthbound. I have no reliable knowledge as to the rate at which relief is reaching these people; but the important thing to realize is that living human beings can do a great deal to help, and I quote, here, a few instances where a clairaudient friend of mine was able to help some of these people and release them from their unhappy, aimless drifting. (I use the word "earthbound" in this connection to indicate a state where the etheric double has not been shed at death, and the victim is consequently between the two worlds, seeing the physical but being unable to communicate, and not seeing the astral or its inhabitants and so being cut off from that world also.) The main point is, I think, that all those who recognise the possibility of spirit help, and reach out for it, find that help, and the drifting crowds, which are described below, were drifting and lost solely because they had not asked for help.

It is very important that this idea shall be disseminated as widely as possible. It doesn't matter so much even if people won't accept the truth now; but sooner or later they may find themselves in this distressing predicament, and then they will be glad to find that they have in the back of their minds the idea that, if they cry out for help, help will be forthcoming.

Always at death there is somebody to meet the soul as it leaves its physical body—maybe a relation or a close friend, or perhaps some one of the invisibles with whom it has a special tie. But it does not follow that the messenger can make himself seen or heard; that depends upon the extent to which the new arrival had developed his spiritual sight. ...

... I should not like it to be supposed that any one of these poor people is really lost or abandoned. The ruling spirit of the Universe is love, and all these people—yes, and all the people down to the deepest hells are watched over and their progress is noted until the time comes when they have learned the needed lesson, whatever it may be, and are fit to be raised up into the next stage in their journey towards the light. It is the greatest mistake to suppose that any suffering, of whatever nature, is imposed as a punishment in the sense of vengeful retribution. It is only that every cause has its specific effect, and the misuse of man's freewill has painful effects, as the result of which, man evolves slowly towards the light of wisdom.

I know no more now about the conditions in hell than I have indicated in my previous books; it is not a subject upon which a healthy mind will wish to dwell, but it is, I think, important to know how much human beings, living in their physical bodies, can do, and do do, to help in the evacuation of those who have served their time, so to speak, and are ready to move up out of the darkness.

Time and again it has been said to me, "The regeneration of mankind must come through man. It is, I think, the chief failing of all the main religions of the world that they ignore the possibility—nay, rather the imperative necessity—of human cooperation in the work of the angels and messengers of God in raising those who are ready to rise from the lowest strata of the astral.[32]

Death is no more than passing from one room into another.

~ Helen Keller

6
A CONSCIOUS DISSOLUTION
~

Edward C. Randall

Edward C. Randall (1860-1935) was a prominent New York trial lawyer from Buffalo who served on the board of directors of a number of large corporations. Randall became interested in Spiritualism around 1890 after attending a séance. Soon after, he established a home circle comprised of his wife and some close associates including a prominent judge, Dean Stuart of Rochester; the object being to attempt to glean some knowledge about the nature of reality, and in particular, reality after physical death. The purpose was also to help deceased earthbound people to understand their situation so that they might continue their spiritual journey.

The circle sat every week at the Randall family home and shortly after the sittings began Randall met Emily French, a "direct voice" medium in her 60's, also from Buffalo. Emily was from a well-known family and had a reputation in her community as a person of integrity. She sat with the Randall's circle for many years until she passed away in 1912. During the long and dedicated relationship she never charged a cent for her time.

"Direct Voice"[33] is a rare form of mediumship whereby the medium sits quietly and voices manifest in his or her presence ... voices of people who have died.

In 1905, Randall wrote to Isaac K. Funk, a prominent psychic researcher and co-owner of the publishing house Funk and Wagnalls of New York & London, asking him to arrange for Emily French to be scientifically tested. Dr Funk agreed on condition that Mrs. French would come to New York City and conduct sittings every day for two weeks in the homes of people she did not know and surrounded by highly experienced, and in most cases, skeptical observers. Emily, by then seventy-two years old and not in good health, duly travelled to New York and sat with Dr Funk and his associates, night after night, with barely any time to rest after the journey from her home in Buffalo. There, they conducted tests, which confirmed that the voices did not originate in Emily's vocal organs. Her Indian control,[34] Red Jacket, reportedly had a loud masculine voice that could easily have filled a hall, whereas Emily, by that time, was frail and deaf and had a weak heart; yet the sitters could always clearly hear the communicators.

Night after night she produced amazing direct voice phenomena where spirits communicated and told the sitters about their afterlife experiences. Dr Funk published the full results of these detailed tests in his book, *The Psychic Riddle*.[35] In total, Randall and French sat together more than 700 times and Randall stated, "Hundreds, yea thousands [of spirits], have come and talked with me, and to many whom I have invited to participate in the work—thousands of different voices with different tones, different thoughts, different personalities, no two alike; and at times in different languages.

During one sitting a communicator explained:

"Yes, I know that I am no longer an inhabitant of the earth sphere, that I am numbered among the dead; so because I thoroughly understand the great change through which I have passed, the group of spirit people working with you, and controlling conditions on this side, have asked me to speak to you, and through you to all those in sorrow for their dead. You know, of course, that in speaking I am now using my own voice."

Out of the silence, out of the darkness, in a room devoted solely to psychic investigation came those words; one whom the world calls dead was speaking. I have never ceased to be startled when a voice first speaks from the invisible world—so unusual, so marvelous, so wonderful, and yet to me, so natural.

"So much," I said, "of the information that we get from the plane where you now live is general in character, won't you be specially specific and tell us, first, something of your occupation and of the conditions immediately preceding your dissolution?"

"I came," he replied, "from a long line of soldiers. My ancestors fought in the American Revolution, and were among those who aided in establishing your Republic; possibly I inherited a martial spirit. When the first shot was fired by the Confederates, and Lincoln issued his call for volunteers, I was possessed with a desire to enter the army. I had a wife and two children, to whom as I now know, I owed a far greater duty than to my country, but the speech of people, the danger of the nation, the condition of slavery prevailing in the Southern States, and the preparation for war, incited me. With forced words of good cheer, I left brave wife and little children, enlisted, and became a soldier in the Union.

"I will not take the time to tell you of my life in the army, except to speak of the nights in camp when my thoughts went out to those at home, knowing as I did that funds were slowly diminishing. Ever the idea was dominant that the war would be soon over, then there would be the home coming, and the plans I formed to make compensation for my long absence would come to fruition. But the war did not end as battle after battle was fought with success first on one side, then on the other. I participated in many, seeming to bear a charmed life, for while thousands about me fell, I passed unharmed, and so grew fearless."

"Under what circumstances did you meet your end?" I asked.

"It was at Gettysburg," he replied. "I can see and feel it all over again as my mind concentrates on that tragic event. It was the second day of that great fight. I was then a colonel and commanded a regiment in reserve; in front of us the battle roared. Shot and shell filled the air and fell near us, muskets belched forth their fire, the earth seemed to tremble; wounded in great numbers were carried to the rear, and we knew that countless dead lay where they had fallen. We waited, knowing it was only a matter of hours, possibly minutes before the order would come to advance. I looked down the line at blanched faces; we all knew that many would not answer the roll call at night. Still we waited. Suddenly out of the smoke galloped an officer from the general's staff. 'Forward,' came the command.

"There was no faltering now that the hour had come. The column moved. Soon shot and shell fell among us; on we went. All was excitement, fear was gone; we had but one desire, and that was to kill; such is the lust of battle. I recall but little more. We reached the front and saw the gray line charging up the hill toward us, then, oblivion. I now know that I was shot."

"Tell me of returning consciousness and what you saw," I said.

"You must remember," the spirit answered, "that these tragic events occurred nearly half a century ago, and that at that time it had not been discovered that there is another life, a plane as material as the one you now inhabit, where life continues. I had no conception of a hereafter, for with all my religious teaching I had no idea of what or where the future life might be; nor was I at all sure there was one; so you can imagine how startled I was to awake as from a deep sleep; bewildered I got to my feet, and looked down and saw my body among many others on the ground. This was startling. I made a great effort to collect my thoughts and recall events. Then I remembered the awful battle; still I did not then realize I had been shot. I was apart from, still I seemed in some way, held to the body and yet separate and apart from the covering I had thought constituted the body.

"I tried to think and realize my situation. I looked about; others of the seeming dead moved, seemed to stir. Then many of us stood up, and, like me, seemed to emerge from their physical bodies, for their old forms still lay upon the field. I looked at other prostrate bodies, examining many: from each something was gone. Going among them again, I found other bodies inhabited, still living as you would say, though wounded and unconscious.

"Soon I found myself among thousands in a similar mental state. Not one among them knew just what had happened. I did not know then, as I do now, that I always possessed a spirit body composed of material called ether, and that the physical body was only the garment it wore while in the earth life."

"What brought you to the full realization of what had happened?" I asked.

"I am coming to that," he said. "While the passing out of the old body was without pain, it is a terrible thing to drive a strong spirit from a healthy body, tear it from its coverings. It is unnatural, and the sensation following readjustment is awful. In a short time it became easier, but I was still bewildered. It was neither night nor day; about us all was gloom, not a ray of light, nor a star. Something like an atmosphere dark and red enveloped us all, and we waited in fear and silence; we seemed to feel one another's thoughts, or to be more correct, hear one another think. No words were spoken. How long we remained in this state I cannot now tell, for we do not measure time as you do. Soon there was a ray of light that grew brighter each moment, and then a great concourse of men and women with kindly faces came, and with comforting words told us not to fear; that we had made the great change; that death, so-called, only advanced our sphere of life; that we were still living beings, inhabitants now of the first plane beyond the earth; that we would live on forever, and by labor reach a higher mental development; that for us the war was over, we had passed through the valley of death.

"I will not attempt to tell you of the sorrow that came with such a realization, not for myself, for I soon learned that only through death could we progress, and that the personal advantages beyond the physical were greater than those in the physical; it was sorrow for the wife and the babies; their great grief when they learned what had happened, bound me to their condition, and we sorrowed together. I could not progress or find happiness until time had healed their sorrow. If only those in earth life knew that their sadness binds and holds us, and stays our progress and development! After coming with the aid of many friends to full consciousness, and being made to move at will, I followed at first the movements of both armies. I saw the route of Lee's army, the final surrender at Appomattox, and I want to tell you of the great effort of this land in which I live put forth, not only to prevent war, but to bring peace when nations or people are at war, for war has never been right. No taking of human life is ever justifiable.

"This is the first time it has been my personal privilege to get a message through to the world I once inhabited. It has been a great pleasure to tell you something of the sensations during and after the change. There is one experience that I want to relate, for it made a profound impression. One day I saw many people passing into a building having the appearance of a great Temple of Music. I was told I could go in if I desired, —I did. There were assembled, I should judge, five thousand people. They sat with bowed heads in a silence, so absolute that I marveled; turning, I asked one beside me the object of the meeting, and I was told they were concentrating their thoughts, sending out peace vibrations to nations at war. I did not comprehend, but, curious, I waited. Soon above that great company arose a golden cloud that formed and moved as if directed. Having learned that I could go at will, I followed and found the cloudy substance enveloping another battlefield. Again a dark condition with flashes of red, immediately surrounding and above two great armies, for the thoughts of those in battle give out emanations producing such effect. It had substantially the same appearance that prevailed on my awakening. As I watched, the dark condition seemed to change, to dissolve before the peaceful conditions of the light that I had followed, just as mist dissolves before the sun. With the change a better thought filled the minds of those engaged: an inclination to treat more humanly the wounded and the prisoners. This is one of the ways those experienced among us help the mental, as those among you aid the physical; both are equally real.

"Among us are the great who counsel together and work to influence those in authority against war, while others among us, by thought suggestions, help to sustain those poor soldiers forced into battle, either to satisfy the greed, selfishness, and ambition of those in authority, or to defend a nation or the integrity of their country. We know neither the one side nor the other. We see only the suffering of humanity, a mother's mourning, a wife's breaking heart, a child's sobbing. They are all human, and without distinction or class we labor to comfort and help them by mental suggestion. In such work we enter their homes, a great invisible host, and many a heart has been cheered through our ministrations. Other wars will come, unless the thought of those now in authority changes; then a great work will be required of us, for which we are ready."

"This is exceedingly interesting, but just one more word. How does your earth-life appear, after so many years?" I asked.

"How much do you remember of those first years, when as an infant you gazed upon your world?" the man replied. "So it is with me. I have but an indistinct recollection of the events that made up my earth-life: only a memory remains, still enough to make me regret many lost opportunities. I was not then a thinker, only a drifter; I accepted what was told me without question; the result was that I did not develop my mental faculties. This life offers such splendid advantages—my joy of living in the present is so intense, that I seldom think of the earth-life at all. All the trials, sorrows, and sufferings incident to birth and the few years in your physical world, were necessary, and from my present vantage ground the matter of living a few years more or less, the manner of my going were unimportant; it is all forgotten now in the wonderful reality about me. As soon as I came to understand what death was and to what it led, I immediately commenced to complete my education, and build a home for the wife and children, and I am happy to tell you that again we dwell together, for they are all here in this land of happiness and opportunity."[36]

Crazy Horse dreamed and went into the world where there is nothing but the spirits of all things. That is the real world that is behind this one, and everything we see here is something like a shadow from that one.

~ BLACK ELK

7
ABOVE THE BATTLEFIELDS

Elsa Barker

Many inspired writings over the years have claimed to have originated from disincarnate beings and Elsa Barker was no exception. Elsa was an American author and poet, born in 1869 in Leicester, Vermont, USA. Throughout her life, her poems and short stories were published in various books and magazines.

She encountered automatic writing (as described in chapter 1 by Wellesley Tudor-Pole) in 1912, when a deceased entity began to write through her hand. The entity claimed to be judge David Patterson Hatch,[37] a lawyer and judge from Los Angeles who had passed away earlier that year.

The judge explained that, having passed over, he wanted to document his afterlife experiences in the form of letters, which he would write through Elsa's hand. Within a few days, Elsa received confirmation from a friend who knew the judge, that he had indeed recently passed away in Los Angeles.

Between 1913 and 1918, more than 130 letters were "dictated" by the judge to Elsa. At his request, they were later published as a trilogy: *Letters from a Living Dead Man, War Letters from the Living Dead Man* and *Last Letters from the Living Dead Man.*[38]

With World War I in full swing, Hatch relayed his observations to Elsa about the horrors of the war from his vantage point in the astral.

Picture to yourself a battlefield, a long-stretching irregular double line of men and guns and horses and all the paraphernalia of war. In the old days on earth, I once gave some study to the theory and practice of war, but that labor had little value in preparing me to study this war. Not only did it take for granted conditions that no longer exist, but my point of observation then was an imaginary station on one side or the other of an imaginary field; now I am really here, there and everywhere. I read the thoughts of the commanders on both sides, I am with the men in the trenches sometimes half-buried in mud and water, I am riding with the cavalry, I go forward with the guns of the artillery and I go out and up with the escaping spirits of the dead—go with them into the hell of confusion that almost always swallows them for a time after they are violently thrust from their bodies.

Truly, war is hell! Have no glorious delusions to the contrary, you who dwell in the haunts of peace and babble of what you know not. The horrors do not end when the guns cease firing. The dark and silent night of rain is full of souls in bewilderment and torment. Often one will grope his way hither and thither, seeking to find a trench-mate to whom he had become attached in the *camaraderie* of war—that sweet flower which grows up an ugly stem. Often they live over and over again the rage and madness of the attack; they plunge an imaginary bayonet into the form of an imaginary foe or, if a mass of them are together, and they generally are, they strike recklessly at anything before them, conscious always of an *opposing* force.

The general, of whom I wrote in my last letter, was a man of marked spiritual development; he soon broke away from the entanglements of matter; he was a devotee to whom his country was a god and his emperor a hero to be followed with aspiration. But most men who die on the battlefields are common soldiers who fight because it is the will of the mass behind them. They generally go out into darkness for a time, and most of them wander in darkness and bewilderment for varying periods.

Some, on the contrary, are vividly conscious almost from the hour of death. These may attack the men of the opposing army when they sleep. The dreams of the battlefields are terrible in their intensity. Sometimes again, for in the general confusion distinctions may be quite lost, souls that had believed themselves enemies cling together in the tragic yearning of the dark that separates the worlds of the "invisible." In their great need they do not know their former friends from their former enemies. Another pale flower that grows from the ugly stem of war! The astral forms of men of low development are often found here in shocking distortion, their consciousness only a glimmer, and with no power of feeling anything but pain. No wonder the dreams of the unselfish lovers of humanity are full of horror during these dark nights of the world, for there are many noncombatants in all lands whose hours of sleep are given to a devoted labor for the souls that need help so horribly. There is one man whom you know who bears at this time a burden almost superhuman, and speaks of it to no one.

It is needless for me to say how you yourself spent the nights of many months, and when we bade you cease that labor it was only that you might have more strength for the labor of writing these pages at my dictation. A soul still held in the flesh cannot work all day and all night. That is burning the astral candle at both ends. When you return to the countries now devastated by war, some of your friends will relate to you experiences similar to your own during these terrible months. They who can be used are called upon when the need is greatest, and the need is immense at this time. Realize that those souls in the lower regions of the astral world are actually in space near the ground of the physical planet. Those who hang over the battlefields where they met their fate are still thrilled or horrified by the noise of the battle horns; they can still hear the shriek of shells and feel the shattering force of the explosions. Day in, day out, these unfortunate earthbound ones live over and over again the emotions of war; night after night, they dread the morning when the sounds will begin again. They cannot get away. They are not free merely because their bodies are buried under a few feet of earth, or worse still left unburied.

I advise you to avoid, for some years at least, the actual scenes of these battles. You can go to Switzerland or to the more southern regions of France, but do not stay long in Northern France or Belgium, or in any other place that may be thus affected. The thought world of England is just now troubled, but the layer of astral matter immediately above the earth is not full of the awful emanations of death. Astral forms go there from the more terrible region, but, in order to go, they must have themselves broken away from the immediate scene of their worst suffering. It is easier to protect oneself from sad thought forms than from the distracted astral entities and the "boiling" astral matter that lie above those battlefields.

Why, even the field of Waterloo before this war was not a pleasant place to spend the night. After a lapse of time, you may briefly visit the scenes of these recent battles, for the sake of the practical experience; but do not go there just yet. The best place in Europe for a long period will be the mountains of Switzerland. You should spend much time there. Do you remember telling me how, when a child, you used to see the forms of American Indians on the hills and in the valleys of your native State? They were those who, many years before, had walked those hills and valleys in the sunlight, and were still held in the tenuous matter above that region. The eyes of childhood are sometimes very clear. Above those battlefields of Europe the sensitive eye may see, for many years, the forms of those who will not be able to make their escape. And I do not mean akashic records.[39] War is hell, and the hell does not end with the signing of peace papers.

That is one reason why we want you, and those others who believe in brotherhood, to carry that spirit of brotherhood among the nations that have been at war. You have no conception of the power of a quiet faith in a great and true idea. The man who really loves his fellows has a wider influence than his own immediate circle of friends. The atmosphere around him is permeated with that brotherly love and sensitive souls can feel it. Some day, sail up the Rhine with that sentiment in your heart.[40]

*The weapons of divine justice are blunted by the
confession and sorrow of the offender.*

~ Dante Alighieri

8
A SOUL IN PURGATORY

That same year Hatch dictated another letter to Elsa, this time on the subject of purgatory.

Dare I talk to you of the purgatory to which the rage of battle conducts so many souls that only a little while before walked the earth as men—went on their daily round from house to office, loving their wives and children and exchanging worldly commonplaces in the intervals of work, all unmindful that they were hourly drifting toward the Great Event? Yes, I dare.

We will follow one soul that I myself followed. His story I can reconstruct from memory, for every act of it is stamped upon my mind. No, I do not need brain cells to remember with. Neither will you when you have escaped the prison of your brain cells.

The man was an officer in an English regiment and he was a bachelor. Outwardly he was much like other men, but his consciousness was different. He lived in a world of his own, for he was a reader and a thinker. He was not a very good man. Not *all* Englishmen are good even now when England is at war—you who bristle at any criticism of your beloved maternal island—you who write for me!

This man was not very good because there was so little love in his heart. He was not incapable of love, yet he was unable to awaken love in others, and so was soul-starved. But sometimes he was conscious of a great yearning, and when the yearning came he was impatient, and took a drink, or cursed his servant, or both. Sometimes when he was most impatient with the world and with himself, he went on a "spree."

The war began. His natural impatience found something congenial in the hurry and noise of the expedition. He was glad to go. He had known a German in London and had disliked him thoroughly. The German talked too much and his loud tones jarred on the sensitive ears of the refined officer. As he led his men into battle he thought of this German. He felt that he was battling with him at last face to face, and the feeling gave him a thrill of satisfaction. Hate had become an almost sensual luxury. The German had fascinated by his blustering personality a woman of rather coarse type to whom the officer had been impatiently attracted. He hated himself for the attraction, and he hated the German for frustrating it. We always hate those who frustrate the emotions we hate. The officer was killed by a German bullet in the early days of the war. Where? Oh, no matter where. There are those who might recognize the man, and I am not a betrayer of unwilling confidences. When I listen at the keyhole of life I never report too much of what I hear. I use my discretion. I shall call this man my friend, for I was so much his friend that I have a right to claim him.

Before the battle in which my friend met death I had lingered near him with a desire to soften the hard feelings in his heart. Those feelings are not usual among the soldiers of a particular section of the northern battle line. To them, fighting is a sort of glorified sport, or it was so last September.

My friend was an exception and that is why I choose to write about him, that my assertion of his exceptional qualities may keep the reader from shuddering too much. I should not like my readers to feel that their friends went through a similar experience. You who hang above this page, my friend was not your friend. The experiences of your friends were less terrible. They were all better men than he, because you loved them, and this man was not good because he was not loved enough. He met death by a rifle bullet. Then all became dark before him, and he was unconscious for a time. He was awakened by the noise of a bursting shell.

"The battle has begun," he thought. "Damn that man! He should have awakened me at dawn." He was among the men of his regiment. They seemed larger than usual, and blurred in outline. He rubbed his eyes. "Hell and damnation! Who have they put in my place?" For he saw a minor officer who commanded where he had commanded.

He turned away, then came back again. He would demand to know! He started toward the place where his superior officer should have been, some distance away, and found himself *instantly* there. "What is the matter with me?" he thought. "Have I lost my mind?" He saluted the officer, who paid no attention to him. "Am I asleep?" he wondered.

"He went up to a soldier who was loading a rifle and touched him on the arm. The soldier also paid no attention. He gripped the man's arm. Still he paid no attention but raised his rifle and fired. My friend went toward two men who were talking together. "Poor old—" he heard one of them say. "Shot through the heart! He was a good officer, though a surly fellow. I'm sorry he's dead."

The man they spoke of was himself.

"Shot through the heart—a good officer—a surly fellow—dead!" He knew. Knowledge sometimes comes more slowly. He was "dead." "Just my luck!" was his instinctive thought. Another shell burst behind him with a shattering report. Suddenly he saw before him a face that riveted his attention. It was a malignant, an insolent face. Then it changed into the face of his enemy, the German back in England whom he hated. "So it's you, is it?" he asked. The specter made no answer but changed its shape again. This time it was like the woman whom my friend had hated himself for liking.

"You, too!" he said, impatiently. Again the specter changed countenance. It was like a servant whom my friend had cursed once too often, and who had left him the year before.

"Are you, too, dead?" he asked, but the face before him had now resumed its original appearance. It was merely a malignant, insolent face, resembling nobody in particular. "What are you, anyway?" my friend demanded; but still there was no answer.

The eye of the specter interested him—the left eye. As he gazed at it the eye gradually enlarged until it seemed the size of a target in a shooting gallery. The iris, of a peculiar greenish-blue, was in the very middle of the eye, so that the white showed all round. The black pupil stared at him with its concentrated malice—a pupil large as a saucer.

"Why do you do that?" demanded my friend, but the eye still made no answer. Then it vanished. A troop of hateful shades came in its place, ugly shades, some human, and some sub-human. Another shell burst nearby, and the shades began to dance. They caught at him and whirled him around with them, around and around until he was dizzy. Then suddenly they stopped, and each and all of them changed into the form of the German back in England whom my friend had hated. Then another group of mad beings mingled with them. They also changed suddenly—there were a dozen duplicates of the woman whom my friend had hated himself for liking, and they and the duplicates of his enemy caught one another's hands and kissed each other.

Sick, revolted, my friend wished himself away, and he was away. He was over among the soldiers of the German army across the plain. He heard the sounds of the language he disliked. "What the devil!" he thought, and the devil stood before him, hoofs, horns and tail complete.

"Hadn't thought of me before, had you?" sneered the evil being. My friend was hurt and bewildered by the appearance, for it looked, with all its unlovely accessories, so like himself.

"Will you, too, change form in a moment?" he asked.

"Oh, no! I change slowly. I only change as you change."

"What do you mean?"

"You only can change me."

"Change, then!" said my friend, but the demon remained as before.

"Change!" repeated my friend, but still the figure before him changed not at all. "Then you lied when you said I could change you!"

"I said that I change slowly."

"What do you mean?"

"I only change as you change."

"And I have not changed, then?"

"It is my business to keep you from changing."

In company with his devil my friend now went through scenes which I refrain from describing, Goethe in the *Walpurgis Night*[41] having done it so well before me. Reckless, desperate, he followed his leader until he was weary and exhausted. Days, weeks passed away, like a nightmare.

"Can I never get rid of you?" he asked his companion.

"Yes, you can get rid of me."

"How?"

"By getting rid of yourself."

"That's easier said than done."

"Yes, that's easier said than done."

Often they found themselves on the battlefield in the fighting line, or at the mess of the soldiers. The smell of the coffee and the cooking meats brought temporary satisfaction to my friend. He tried to drink from brandy flasks tilted to the mouths of men who could not see him or protest; he steeped himself in hungers and despairs. His companions were always changing themselves into the forms of the man he hated and the woman he loved. He witnessed their coarse lovemaking. Sometimes the simulacrum of the woman turned to him with a friendly word. He cursed her, but clung to her hand. But always she vanished when his mouth yearned to hers. Sometimes in a great battle the rage of war awoke in him. He hurled himself at the men of the opposing army, as if he would take revenge upon them for all he was suffering. He struggled to tear the rifles from their hands, and, when one of them passed out of the body, he tried to awake him from the darkness and the sleep into which he was sinking; but never could he succeed in doing this. Never could he succeed in doing anything. His very existence was failure and futility and discouragement.

One day I came to him and touched him on the forehead.

"You are not like these others," he said, dully. "Where do you come from?"

"I came from a distance," I said. "Would you like to go with me?"

"Anywhere away from here," he assented.

"Do you want to be alone?"

"No. It is worst when I am alone."

"The worst is over," I said.

"What do you mean?"

"I mean that you have exhausted, for the time, the springs of your lower desires. You are weary and disgusted with the life you have led since you escaped your body."

"That is a strange expression—escaped! It is only now that I long to escape."

"And it is I that will help you to escape from another layer of your prison, another skin of the onion that shuts you in."

"And why do you do this?"

"To spare you unnecessary fumbling to break the skin," I said. "Would you like to go to sleep?"

"I should like to rest a little."

While he slept I helped to loosen him further, and, when he awoke into another and freer world, I was still with him.

"What would you like to see?" I asked.

"Something beautiful," he answered, "something beautiful and pure."

"Would you care to witness a dance of elves?" I asked, smiling.

"A dance of elves? Are there really such things?"

"The universe contains innumerable forms of life and consciousness," I said, "and you who believe in devils from experience can surely believe in elves."

They came toward us as I spoke, lithe, tenuous forms, dancing with joy across the flowery spaces of the Elysian Fields. They swayed and circled around us, those beings pure as the air in which they moved, light as the happiness they exhaled, enduring as hope and lovelier than mortal dreams. The shadows had all gone from my friend's face, and he, too, seemed to taste joy; he, too, was light as air, and pure. He joined their dance and circled with them around me.

I tell you in a burst of confidence that I also have danced with elves. This companion and friend of the Beautiful Being has swum in the sea of universal life and floated on the wings of irresponsibility. He who knows too much of the world's sorrow must sometimes lighten the load by knowing nothing but joy. When the sylphs had gone to their more inviolable retreat, another shape came toward us.

"What would you like to see now?" I asked him.

"Can I see a person who still lives in England?" he asked, half shyly, yet with the winning confidence of souls who trust their own desires—the higher wisdom which comes with the purification of desire.

"Perhaps," I said. The form that came toward us was unfamiliar to me, but my friend recognized and welcomed it. A woman of intense and vital personality, yet with that purity of atmosphere without which no communion is possible in the region where we then were, was standing beside my friend.

"Let us sit together a little," I said. "It will seem more homelike."

The two beside me seemed happy in each other's presence. Sisterly-sweet hand in hand, they sat together, and though I knew that one of them was only the simulacrum of a living woman, yet she also seemed real to me for the moment, for the kind sentiments of the heart *are* real, and, in the region to which I had conducted my friend, all sentiments are kind. No enemies are found there, and the woman he liked also liked him, or she could not have been there.

Soon I left them in each other's company and went back to the labors of the battlefield; for there were others who needed me, and my friend was safe for the time. After a while I shall help him onward to an experience still less restricted. We take an interest in those whom we have helped, and wish to help them further. Why did I choose this man for my friendly ministrations, you are wondering; for, as I described him in the beginning of this letter, he was not an attractive character. I tell you a little secret; it was because he was unattractive that I chose him. No one had ever loved him enough, and so he needed help more than others. Those who are loved are already helped by that love. As the Beautiful Being says, "Do you get my meaning, daughter of earth?" Just now I live to serve mankind through the horrors of this war. Serve also by loving those who least attract your love. So shall you learn the way to the Path where walk the Masters of Compassion.[42]

God calls and you do not hear, for you are preoccupied with your own voice.

~ A Course in Miracles

9
SELFISHNESS

Carl A. Wickland

Dr. Carl A. Wickland (1861-1945) was a member of the Chicago Medical Society, the American Association for the Advancement of Science and chief psychiatrist at the National Psychopathic Institute of Chicago. Wickland specialized in cases of schizophrenia, paranoia, depression, addiction, manic-depression, criminal behavior and other phobias.

After moving to Los Angeles in 1918, he founded the National Psychological Institute of Los Angeles with his wife Anna Wickland, who was a trance medium.

Wickland treated many patients suffering from mental illness of all kinds, and, after many years experience, came to the conclusion that a number of patients whom he treated had "attachments;" by that he meant that spiritual entities had attached themselves to unwitting patients and influenced them (often) in the worst kind of way, leading them to alcoholism, madness, and occasionally murder.

He stated at the time;

> Spirit obsession is a fact, a perversion of a natural law, and is amply demonstrable. This has been proven hundreds of times by causing the supposed insanity or aberration to be temporarily transferred from the victim to a psychic sensitive who is trained for the purpose, and by this method we ascertain the cause of the psychosis to be an ignorant or mischievous spirit, whose identity may frequently be verified.

Having come to the "spirit obsession" conclusion, Wickland and his wife set up a rescue circle, with Mrs. Wickland acting as the medium, and they set about communicating with lost souls who had passed away and were unaware of their post-physical death condition, and often in denial due to dogmatic religious and equally dogmatic atheist beliefs.

During a rescue sitting in October 1916, a communicator came through who identified himself as William Stead,[43] the renowned British journalist and Spiritualist who had drowned on the *Titanic* four years earlier in 1912.

October 22, 1916.
Spirit: John J. A.
Psychic: Mrs. Wickland.

After the spirit of W. T. Stead had visited with us a few moments, another spirit came in, struggling desperately, as if swimming, and called loudly for aid.

SELFISHNESS

Spirit. "Help! Help!"

Doctor Wickland. "Where did you come from?"

Sp. "That man who just left told me to come in here."

Dr. "Have you been in the water?"

Sp. "I drowned, but I have come to life again. I cannot see that man now, but I heard him talking and he told me to step in. He said that you know the way and would teach me, and that I could go with him afterwards. But now I cannot see him. I'm blind! I'm blind! I don't know whether the water blinded me or not, but I am blind."

Dr. "That is only spiritual blindness. When a person passes out of his physical body without a knowledge of the laws of the higher life, he finds himself in a condition of darkness. It is the darkness of ignorance."

Sp. "Then I will not always be blind?"

Dr. "You must realize that you are in the spirit world and that spirit friends are here who will teach you how to progress out of your condition of darkness."

Sp. "I can see a little now. For a while I could see, but the door was shut again and I could not see through. I was with my wife and child for a time, but no one noticed me. But now the door is closed and I am out in the cold. I am all alone when I go to my home. Changes seem to have taken place. I do not know what I shall do."

Dr. "You have not realized your own situation."

Sp. "What is the matter anyway? What is causing this darkness? What can I do to get out of it? I never was so handicapped as I am now. I was all right for just a minute. I hear somebody talking. There, now I see him again. Was it Mr. Stead?"

Dr. "Mr. Stead was speaking through this instrument [the medium, Mrs. Wickland] just before you came. Mr. Stead probably brought you here for help. It is our work to awaken earthbound spirits who are in darkness."

Sp. "This darkness is terrible. I have been in this darkness for a long time."

Dr. "Understand that there is no death. Life continues in the spirit world, where each one must serve others in order to progress."

Sp. "I really was not what I should have been. I just lived for self. I wanted amusement and to spend money. But now all I have seen is my past, and I have been in the darkness, and it is terrible. Every act of my past stands before me, and I want to run away from it, but I cannot. It is there all the time and accuses me, because I could have done differently. I have seen so many places where I could have done good, but now it seems too late."

Dr. "When a person lives for self alone he usually finds himself in darkness when he passes over to the other side of life. You must obtain understanding of the glories of the spirit world and realize that life there is service to others. That is the true 'Heaven'—it is a condition of mind."

Sp. "Why are not these things taught in the world?"

Dr. "Would the world listen? Humanity as a whole does not look for the spiritual side of life but looks for other things. The world is seeking for amusement and for selfish gain, not for truth."

Sp. "There is such a queer feeling coming over me! Mother! Mother my loving mother! (Spirit.) I am a man, but I feel like a child in your arms again. I have been longing for you, but I have been living all by myself in the terrible darkness. Why is it that I should be in the dark? Cannot my eyes be cured? Will I be blind all the time? Isn't it strange that I can see you, yet I seem to be blind?"

Dr. "You have a spiritual body now, and when your spiritual eyes are opened you will see the beautiful things of the spirit world."

Sp. "I see Mr. Stead there. We were both on the same boat but he does not seem to be in the dark."

Dr. "He understood the truth of spirit return and life on the other side while he was on earth. Life is a school and we must learn all we can about the spirit side of life while we are on earth, for the only light we have when we pass to the other side is the knowledge pertaining to life's problems which we have gathered here."

Sp. "Why did no one ever tell me these things?"

Dr. "Would you have listened to any one who would have tried to talk to you on these subjects?"

Sp. "No one ever approached me with such ideas."

Dr. "What year do you think this is?"

Sp. "1912."

Dr. "It is 1916."

Sp. "Where have I been? I have been very hungry and cold. I had a very great deal of money, but lately when I have wanted some to spend I could not get hold of it. Sometimes I seemed to be shut up in a room, very dark, and I could see nothing but a procession of my past life. I was not a bad man, but you probably know what society people are. I did not know until now what it was to be poor. It is a new experience to me. Why should humanity not be taught differently before death? Then there would not be such suffering as I am in now."

Dr. "If you will go with your mother and other spirit friends and try to understand what they tell you, you will feel much happier."

Sp. "I can see Mr. Stead. I met him on the boat but I had no use for his teachings. I thought he was old and that he had a hobby. You know when people get old they have hobbies of one kind or another. I never had time for such things, because all I thought of was my money and society. We do not see the poor people and we do not care to see them. I could do so differently now, but money is of no use to me any longer. My mother is waiting for me and I should like to go with her, for I have not seen her for years, and it is so good to see her. She says she could not reach me, for I was like a crazy man and would not listen to her.

"Bless you all for the help you have been to me, and for having opened my eyes. It is misery to be blind, yet able to see the procession of your past life, and not be able to see or hear anything else."

Dr. "We should like to know your name."

Sp. "I am John J. A., and I am glad I met you all. I am so grateful for what you have told me. Now I can see and hear, and understand something that I did not know existed. My mother and friends are coming for me, and now I am going through that beautiful gate into what will be to me heaven.

"I again thank you all, and hope some day to come and see you again.

Goodbye."

~

Dr. Wickland used initials in his book to protect the identity of the communicators who may have had family who were still living at that time.

John J. A. said he was on the same "boat" as Stead, the *Titanic*. There was only one John J. A on the passenger list[44] of victims aboard the *Titanic* and that was John Jacob Astor IV,[45] who, at the time, was one of the richest people in the USA. The John. J. A. communicator fits Astor's description. He talks about having a great deal of money, being part of society, and his "loving mother." In Richard Grant's article on Astor, "The House That Jack Built,[46] Grant writes, "He (Astor) was devoted to his domineering mother, who had pampered him thoroughly."

A few weeks later, John J. A. brought a friend, another member of New York's aristocracy, who had met his death at the sinking of the *Lusitania*.

November 5, 1916
Spirit: Alfred V.
Psychic: Mrs. Wickland.

Spirit. "Somebody told me to come in here and I would get warm."

Dr Wickland. "What is your name?"

Sp. "Alfred V. I was on a boat. John J. A. came and told me he would try to help me get in here. He said if I would come in here I would get help. Say, I have never been hungry in my life before, but I am both hungry and cold, and my clothes are all wet."

Dr. "That is only a condition of your mind. You have lost your physical body and should not feel the need of food."

Sp. "I know I drowned and I have been in misery ever since."

Dr. "If you had an understanding of the life hereafter and of progression in the spirit world you would soon find happiness through serving others."

Sp. "I never was happy. I suppose I had my own way too much, yet sometimes I felt, what was the use. But I thought: Just forget yourself and have a good time. You may not care for society life, but in society you can drown yourself in gaiety. I really did not care for society life. I used to forget myself with my horses. If you have a beautiful horse he is faithful to you through life. But when you get into society, women just show you one side smiles, and sometimes they hate you. The love I know most is the love of a beautiful, faithful horse. Horses were my pleasure and I felt they loved me. Women liked me only for what I could do for them; they wanted money and pleasure. Women wanted all the money they could get from me. I let go of things and tried to lose myself in pleasure, but I was not happy.

"Society does not know anything about honor and respectability. If I could find people as faithful and true as my horse was to me, I tell you I would thank you for that society. But go into the kind of society I have known, and men and women are nothing.

"I was a sport myself, but there were things that drove me to forget that little thing within me, conscience. I longed for something that was good, but where can you find it? Not amongst society, but amongst horses. Society is all right if you want that kind of a life. You will probably realize that I developed a great deal of selfishness."

Dr. "You must try now to forget your past life with all its sorrow and bitterness. Look for higher things; then your spiritual eyes will be opened."

Sp. "Friends that took an interest in me brought me here, and my eyes have been opened since I came. I feel that but I am not sure a time may come when I can be happy. I have never been really happy, for when a child I had my own way too much.

I thank you for allowing me to come here. If I ever am truly happy I will come back and tell you so."

The only victim on the passenger list of the *Lusitania*[47] with the initials Alfred V. was Alfred Vanderbilt (October 20, 1877–May 7, 1915),[48] a New York born sportsman, socialite, and member of the Vanderbilt family.[49]

A sequel to the above occurred two years later, when John J. A., and Alfred V., brought to our circle a friend of theirs, Anna H., a stage celebrity.

SELFISHNESS

September 8, 1918
Spirit: Anna H.
Psychic: Mrs. Wickland.

Spirit "Water! Please, water! (A glass of water was given and eagerly taken.) Thank you so much! I have been very sick and am still weak. The doctors really do not know what is the matter with me. They said I must be kept quiet. My legs and arms pain me so."

Doctor "We will relieve your pain." (Manipulating arms of psychic.)

Sp. "Be very careful about my bones. I want to retain my beautiful form. I want to get well and return to my work. I have been very sick, and I am still very weak."

Dr. "What is your name?"

Sp. "My name is Anna H."

Dr. "How did you come to Los Angeles?"

Sp. "I am not in Los Angeles. I am in New York."

Dr. "Who brought you here?"

Sp. "I thought I had a dream and that Alfred V. came and spoke to me. He always liked me, but he is dead. Now he says that I must wake up.

I am so sick. My bones, my bones! I don't want to lose my beautiful form. I feel that I am commencing to get better and stronger. Will I live now, and can I perform again and do my work? I do not want to lose my beautiful form."

Dr. "You will never perform on the physical plane again."

Sp. "I hope to. Alfred V. bothered me so much, but he is dead."

Dr. "Does he look as though he were dead?"

Sp. "He seems to be very well, but I thought I was dreaming. Why, here is John J. A., too! They are both dead."

Dr. "So are you."

Sp. "When did I die?"

Dr. "A short time ago."

Sp. "Alfred says that they do missionary work to wake up spirits. But they do not believe in such things as spirits. I don't want to die."

Dr. "Nobody actually 'dies.'"

Sp. "Of course they do. The doctors said I could never get well. I fought and fought to live. I want to live. I want to overcome my sickness and get well again, and I want to retain my beautiful form."

Dr. "From now on you must try to develop a beautiful spirit."

Sp. "The two men want me to go with them to find understanding."

Dr. "They have found the truth through this little circle. They were very poor spiritually before they came here, but became rich, through an understanding of a more beautiful life than they had here on earth."

Sp. "What is this place? They say it is the Gate to the Understanding of Real Life—The Gateway."

(Noticing Mrs. Wickland's dress.) "This dress does not fit well. (Touching neck and shoulders.) This is not my neck, or face, or form. They say I am weak yet, but I am to go with them and they will show me the way, but that I have much to learn."

Dr. "Did you ever ask yourself: 'What is Mind?'"

Sp. "No. I just wanted my beautiful form. If it were not for my beautiful form and acting I could not have attracted people to me and earned my living. There are quite a few people here. (Spirits.) Alfred said if I came here he would bring me to my relations, and to a beautiful home beyond the grave."

Dr. "What do they call that place?"

Sp. "I do not like the name, but they say, 'The Spirit World.' They say that is the home beyond the grave.

SELFISHNESS

They say I shall have to overcome my earthly condition before I can open my psychic eyes. I do not know what they mean. They say if I go with them I will find beautiful conditions after I have understanding, but that I shall have to overcome a great deal of self and live for others.

"Alfred says that we lived for society and ourselves, and we have to suffer for it. He says I must go, but I cannot, for I am very sick."

Dr. "Your body was sick, but you have lost that body. It is in the East."

Sp. "I feel better now than I did a while ago."

Dr. "My wife is a psychic sensitive, and you are speaking through her body. Alfred V. and John J. A. at one time controlled her body as you are now doing."

Sp. "My bones are so sore."

Dr. "That is only in your mind. Mind is not the body. Mind is invisible. We do not see you at all; you are invisible to us."

Sp. (Touching face.) "This is not my face, and I don't want this form. I want my beautiful form."

Dr. "It will be your duty to serve others in the spirit world."

Sp. "These people want me to go with them. They took quite an interest in me and my work. My pains seem to be leaving me. Will you please tell me how I could come here when you are all strangers to me? I do not know why I should be here tonight. I feel so well now."

Dr. "We are carrying on experimental work to learn what becomes of the dead. My wife is a psychic and you are controlling her body."

Sp. "Alfred says I must go. I thought I had a dream and that I was going to die, but I fought and fought for a long time. I did not want to die, so I used all my will power to live as long as I could.

"One day I felt very weak and I went to sleep for quite a while, but I woke up again, as I wanted to live. They thought I was dead, but I was not. I had only gone to sleep. I wanted to live because life is dear to me, but I was sick so long and suffered so severely.

"I went to sleep again and I slept a long time, and when I woke up it was all dark, and I could not see anything at all. Everything was dark, dark, dark. I could not find any light and it was so dark. I felt so distressed—all dark.

"I thought then I went to sleep again, and as I slept I dreamed Alfred V. and John J. A. came to me and said: "Anna, wake up! We are here to help you. Come with us. Come!" I thought I was waking up, but I was so sick, so sick, that I could not go with them. My crippled body was so sick.

"They said: "We will take you to a place where you will have a new body, and you will be well and strong. Come with us to a more beautiful world than this." Here I am, all well and strong. Will I not have those terrible pains again? They are so hard on me.

I felt I must not eat too much, or drink too much, or I would not be able to retain my beautiful form. I would not eat meat, because I would get too fat, and I must eat just enough to retain the roundness of my form.

"What have I now? Why did I not do more helpful things? Life was so sweet. I liked to be flattered and I liked to have admirers. It is so hard to lose your admirers."

Dr. "Do Alfred V. and J. A. flatter you now?"

Sp. "No. They do not look as they used to. There is a seriousness about them. They look so sincere that I feel different with them. While to me they look much younger, I know they are older. They do not say to me as they did once: "Come along and have a good time."

SELFISHNESS

Life was very sweet while I had admirers. But I suffered for my vanity.

The doctors said if I had not laced so much I would not have been so sick. I would not mind the doctors either. They wanted me to eat to get strength, but I was afraid if I lay there and ate, and did not get my regular massage and baths, I could not keep my form, so I starved myself.

"When I was in the dark, Alfred came to me and said: "Come I will show you something far more beautiful than a beautiful form and selfishness and vanity. They are only shadows. Now come, and we will show you why we should live for others. "You will be beautiful again when you have served others, but you must forget self and overcome all selfishness." Now I must serve and I must help."

Suddenly the spirit lost control and was gone.

Anna H. might well have been Anna Held,[50] a Polish born Broadway performer who lived in New York. Anna Held died of multiple myeloma on August 12th, 1918, just three weeks before the Anna H. communication.

*Life is indestructible;
it is beyond time and space,
therefore death can only change its form,
arrest its manifestation in this world.*

~ Leo Tolstoy

10
ONE DAY AS A THOUSAND YEARS

Elsa Barker

In *War Letters from a Living Dead Man*, Judge David Patterson Hatch continued dispensing his wisdom to Elsa. In this letter he gives some comfort to the bereaved.

As I am writing about war, I wish to talk to those who have lost their loved ones in this war. You who grieve for the untimely dead, have you not read that one day shall be as a thousand years and a thousand years as one day? We must start on the basis of re-birth, whose other name is rhythm, and whose course is immortality. Immortality presupposes no beginning and looks forward to no end. The spirit always was and always will be. In the life of the spirit, one day is as a thousand years and a thousand years are as one day. Birth is the morning of a new day, and death is the evening of that day, and the period between lives is the period of sleeping and dreaming. Or you may turn it the other way and say that life is a dream and death the awakening to reality. But the rhythm is sure.

Falling asleep is a passing through the astral world, much as a soul passes through it after death. You who write for me and a few others pass through it in full consciousness. Some day all men will pass through it consciously and will bring back the memory. You who grieve for the dead, remember that a lifetime is but a day to the immortal spirit. Often have you parted from a loved one for a day and felt no grief there at.

The loved one left home to perform a duty and you felt sure that the next day you would see him again. Can you not feel that in the next day of the soul, the next lifetime (it is all the same in eternity), you will greet your loved one again? Friends do not meet in every life unless they are very intimate. As you often do not see one friend or another more than once a week, so in the greater days of the soul you may not meet all your friends every day. You part from one on Monday with a definite engagement to meet on Friday. Four days, four lifetimes, it is all the same in eternity.

But from some you only part for a few hours, from noon to sunset, and meet again in the evening in the intimacy of home. Those who have left you now in the midday of life will perhaps come home to you at the sunset; which is only another way of saying that they may meet you at the end of this day of the soul, the end of this life, and be with you in the twilight period of the astral life and in the sweet dream of heaven beyond. Do not grieve. Love waits for its own. Some friends you may meet again two, four or seven lifetimes away, but those who are really your intimates, your lovers, your own, you will meet again at the sunset, or at the latest tomorrow—the next day of the soul on earth.

How will you prepare for the meeting? Will you not work cheerfully all day, knowing that at dusk love will come back to you? As sunset approaches, will you not robe yourself in the white garment of faith, the evening garment, and watch for love at the window? Love will come.

Can you not in anticipation hear his footstep on the gravel? Can you not hear the click of the lifted latch? Will you not go forward with a smile to greet love? Surely, one day shall be as a thousand years and a thousand years as one day.

I took counsel with the soul of an English officer who died in leading a charge. His death was quick and painless. A shot through the heart and he found himself after a period of unconsciousness, still as he supposed, leading a charge. But there was no enemy before him, nothing but the tranquil fields above the tumult, for so great was his exaltation of spirit—he had died with the thought of his love in his heart-—that he had gone up and up to the region where love may have room. Seeing nothing before him he paused, looked round and saw me.

"Brother," I said, "You have left the war behind you." He understood.

Those who have lived for weeks in the tents of death are not slow in recognizing death when he lifts the curtain.

"And what of the charge?" he asked eagerly. "Was the charge won?"

"Yes," I replied, "the force of your spirit won it."

"Then all is well," was his answer.

"Rest a little," I said. "Rest and talk with me."

"Have we met before?" he asked. "For your face is familiar to me."

"My face is familiar to many on the battlefields," I said.

"When did you come ... out here?"

"Three years ago."

"Then you can teach me much."

"Perhaps I can teach you something. What do you want to know?"

"I would know how to comfort one to whom my death will bring great grief."

"Where is she?" I asked. He named the place. "Then come," I said, "I will go with you."

We found a beautiful woman in a little room in England, a little room that contained a little bed. And in the bed was a boy four or five years old. We could hear the voices of the mother and child as they talked together.

"And when will father come home?" the little one asked.

"I do not know," said the mother.

"Father will come home, won't he? Are you sure that he will come home?"

"I pray that he comes home soon," was all the mother said.

The eyes of children, as they pass into the twilight world, the world between waking and sleeping, are sometimes very clear.

"Why, father has come home!" the child cried, and he stretched out his arms to the father with a glad cry. And the mother knew and was very still. But her grief was softened by knowing that he whom she loved had come home and that her child had seen him. I think he will remain with her until she can join him here. The delay will not retard the progress of his soul. Love is the fulfilling of the law. There is time in eternity for love and the delays of love. In love a thousand years are as one day.[51]

*And you will know the truth,
and the truth will set you free.*

~ JOHN 8:31-32

CONCLUSION

Although this chapter is titled "Conclusion," when it comes to the age-old question, "what happens after we die?" I don't think many of us, if any, can conclude with any certainty what actually happens. All we can do is look at the evidence.

If we assume for a moment that the communicators in this book are genuine, what are we to glean from what they tell us? One thing we can say is, that it seems our state of mind when we physically die is very important because our state of mind prior to death appears to influence our transition to what comes next.

As shown by NDE reports, the absence of belief in an afterlife doesn't preclude an NDE although it's interesting to note that 85% of children experience them as opposed to 4 - 15% of adults. Even if these statistics are approximate, the difference between children and adults is stark.

When Jesus said: "Truly I tell you, unless you change and become like little children, you will never enter the kingdom of heaven" (Matthew 18:3), maybe what he was saying was, being humble, open minded, non-judgmental and loving is more important than any doctrine or belief.

I could never understand the idea of "deathbed repentance" that some Christians espouse: *Repentance*: noun*:* "The action of repenting; sincere regret or remorse." How could suddenly regretting something on one's deathbed make everything okay? It didn't make sense to me. But then I discovered that the word *repent* in the Bible was translated from the word, *metanoia*: Late 19th century: from Greek, from *metanoein* to "change one's mind."

To "change one's mind" feels very different from expressing regret. To change one's mind—to have a "light bulb moment," and realize our previous thoughts and actions might have been incorrect, might well help us after we've died, and, even if it happens on our deathbed, that might be better than not changing one's mind at all.

In 1916 during the Wickland sittings (chapter 9) the communicator calling himself John J. A. was clearly traumatized and feeling desperately cold. He had died on the *Titanic* in 1912 and yet, four years later, he still thought he was in a damp, cold place. He appeared to be experiencing a never-ending nightmare ... hell, some might call it, in part because he didn't realize he was dead, or at least he didn't understand his situation. He hadn't experienced *metanoia*.

John J. A. talked about his self-centered lifestyle; "I just lived for self," he said. "I wanted amusement and to spend money. But now all I have seen is my past, and I have been in the darkness, and it is terrible." He seemed to be suggesting that his post-death environment was a result of his physical life. Why should a self-centered life lead to suffering after death? There are plenty of decent, honest, nice, but self-absorbed people so why should they suffer? Maybe it's because they are so bound up in their physical lives, that after they die they have to unbind themselves and that might take as long as it takes.

Alfred V. apparently had been on the *Lusitania*, the ship that had been sunk by a German U-boat on May 5, 1915, with the loss of 1198 passengers. Alfred was brought to Wickland and his mediumistic wife on November 5, 1916, eighteen months after his death, and although he was aware he had drowned, he still felt cold and hungry and complained that *his clothes were wet*.

Meanwhile, Stead, who guided John J. A. to the Wicklands, seemed perfectly fine. Stead, being a Spiritualist, was convinced that physical death wasn't the end, therefore he would have expected to be somewhere after death, whereas John J. A. and Alfred V. weren't open to the idea of an afterlife and they struggled.

There's a saying, "You are what you eat," ... well, after physical death it appears "we are what we think," therefore, while we're physically living, being open to survival of death might be a better idea than remaining close-minded and denying such a thing is possible.

That said, Private Dowding (no relation to Lord Dowding) in chapter 1, communicating through Wellesley Tudor-Pole during World War I, was convinced he wouldn't survive his physical death and yet said that he had a relatively easy transition after being killed by a piece of shrapnel. Although, like John, he regretted having lived a selfish life; "Live widely," he advises. ...

"Books appealed to me more than life or people. I am now suffering for my mistakes."

In chapter 2, Lord Dowding shared a communication with a New Zealander who had been helped by Colonel Gascoigne. The colonel, having passed away in 1937, like Stead, seemed to be helping dead soldiers to understand their situation by guiding them to his wife and daughter, who were both still alive and appeared to have mediumistic gifts: at least one of them did.

The New Zealander appeared to be a little confused after dying but not unduly stressed. When he said: "I am rather vague as to who is "alive" and who is "dead," they all look much alike," I wonder if the "live' people he was referring to were dreaming while travelling in the astral plane, as we are told we do, or whether the New Zealander was occupying our dimension? That is certainly what seemed to be happening to the Polish pilot in the same chapter, who, having been shot down, found himself wandering among French peasants *who weren't aware of his presence.*

He said he had no faith and as a result felt lost and knew nothing; "What you expect here, that you find—you build your awakening ... I expected nothing, so nothing came."

The communicator in chapter 5 told Edward Randall via medium Emily French that he died on the second day of the Battle of Gettysburg during the American Civil War. He lamented that despite his religious teachings he had no concept of an afterlife. He told the sitters: "... You can imagine how startled I was to awake as from a deep sleep; bewildered I got to my feet, and looked down and saw my body among many others on the ground. This was startling. ... Soon I found myself among thousands in a similar mental state. Not one among them knew just what had happened. ..." He added: "I soon learned that only through death could we progress and that the personal advantages beyond the physical were greater than those in the physical."

Only through death could we progress—it seems such an obvious statement in that context and it's actually very profound—we have to be fit for death, death in itself being a means to an end.

Judge David Patterson Hatch, the *Living Dead Man* using Elsa Barker's hand wrote,

> Realize that those souls in the lower regions of the astral world are actually in space near the ground of the physical planet. Those who hang over the battlefields where they met their fate are still thrilled or horrified by the noise of the battle horns; they can still hear the shriek of shells and feel the shattering force of the explosions.

It appears that once you're dead, knowing you're dead is a great help because a person unaware that they are dead could well experience a nightmarish scenario indefinitely or for *eternity*, to use philosophical parlance, that is, until they *wake up*. The Tibetan Buddhists think so. Rob Nairn at the Agyu Samye Ling Monastery and Tibetan Centre in Scotland wrote in his book, *Living, Dreaming, Dying,*

> When we die, our stream of consciousness floats free and roams the death bardos, undergoing very powerful experiences. In this state a huge potential for liberation is present, because if the person's bardo mind were to focus on its spiritual reality, the realization and experience of that reality would be beyond anything we could imagine from our knowledge of spiritual practice here. The mind is

nine times stronger and the environment in which it moves is less solid than this one. Thus, if it thinks of a place, it will be there. If it is able to focus on spiritual truth it will immediately be drawn into it, experience it and be liberated by it.

In the death bardos our enlightened reality appears to us over and over again, and by now we know the key. If the bardo mind can focus sufficiently to recognize the experience for what it is, instead of fleeing in fear or falling into confusion, the result will be immediate enlightenment.

The death bardos, meaning "intermediate state"—the state between death and rebirth—sound remarkably like the astral plane or paradise, the state where the communicators in the preceding chapters appear to have found themselves after death. In that state, some seemed to be having a heavenly time while others appeared to be experiencing something more hellish.

In Er's near-death experience (if that's what it was), there were judges who decided people's fate depending on their actions on Earth. The judges sat in the "intermediate space" and "bound their sentences in front of them." The just ascended to the heavenly spheres and the unjust descended to the underworld. The symbols of their deeds were "fastened on their backs."

Er also saw people returning from above and below who "went forth with gladness into the meadow" where they embraced and conversed with other spirits before choosing another life and reincarnating. Er was told he was not being judged at that time because he was to go on living and report his findings to his fellow men.

His experience is similar to many modern day accounts although, today, NDErs and spirit communicators, in the main, report that there is no external judgment after death. God is unconditional love, we are told, and if love is unconditional there can be no condemnation.

However, that doesn't mean to say there aren't consequences for our thoughts and actions. During the life review, which so many NDErs experience, every thought and action is shown, good and bad, and every consequence. Many report that the only judging during the review is done by the person whose life is being reviewed. As a result we have to rectify our own transgressions if we are to progress, therefore the judgment process is self-perpetuating.

Michael Tymn,[52] who has written volumes on nineteenth and early twentieth-century mediumship and life after death, echoes the early psychical researcher Robert Hare[53] when he talks about "moral specific gravity," the idea that our *goodness* dictates our environment in the afterlife, therefore there is no need for another being to judge us. They might be onto something.

If a being came to Earth from a planet with a different gravitational pull, and the being was going to jump off a high building, we might advise it that it would be a bad idea to do that because gravity would ensure it hit the ground.

Gravity dictates how we operate here; maybe light does the same there. In other words, light determines our true nature, or rather light *is* our true nature ... we are light beings and the more we spiritually evolve the lighter and brighter we become. The opposite might also be true that the further we are from an unconditional loving state that some call God, the denser and slower our vibration is, and, as a result, darker. We can only go where we can stand the light.

A person living in a state of unconditional love, someone Christ-like or Buddha-like, is what we ultimately need to become if we are to escape the wheel of rebirth; the death bardos; the astral plane, call it what you will, and return home—home being in the light with God, whatever God is.

Forgiveness also seems to play a key part in navigating the afterlife. Religious traditions view forgiveness in high regard but, for many, unconditional forgiveness is a tough thing to accept. Personally, I'm all for it—I think the forgiver always wins. It doesn't have to be about the other person or situation—it's a state of mind. You might be thinking: "Tell that to the parent whose child has been murdered," and of course many of us understandably feel unable or unwilling to forgive, but after death it might be essential if we are to evolve spiritually. We evolve physically here so why should our evolution stop just because we have shed our physical body?

For Jesus, forgiveness was of great importance. Throughout the New Testament he gave many examples, the most well known being The Prodigal Son (Luke 15:11-32),[54] The Lost Sheep (Luke 15:4-7),[55] and The Adulterous Woman (John 8:1-11).[56] During his conversation with Peter he tells him: "I will give you the keys to the kingdom of heaven. Whatever you bind on earth shall be bound in heaven; and whatever you loose on earth shall be loosed in heaven", (Matthew 16:19).[57]

The Norwegian in chapter 2 alluded to the problem of not being able to forgive when he complained; "I was shot by the Germans in Trondheim. I was a little shopkeeper; they shoot. I do not love the Germans. I never shall, but I am held up here by my hatred."

Realizing that his unwillingness to forgive was the cause of his suffering he said: "He [Colonel Gascoigne] tells me that we must forgive the Nazis, that they do not know what they do, that they are like sleep-walkers, and until I forgive them I cannot get free, to pass from

CONCLUSION

this plane so near the Earth on to other planes ..." He continued, "I see why Christ quickly forgave everyone before he left his earth body."

To quote Jesus again, "Whatever you bind on earth shall be bound in heaven."

The Norwegian certainly seemed to be *bound* but hopefully, with the help of Colonel Gascoigne, Mrs. Gascoigne, and others around him, he learned to forgive his enemies and move on.

In John 14:2 Jesus said, "My Father's house has many rooms; if that were not so, would I have told you."[58] That may be so but it appears from the reports in this book that some rooms are better than others.

―

Blaise Pascal, the French mathematician, physicist and philosopher, living in the seventeenth century, suggested that each and every one of us has made a bet as to whether God exists or not. Pascal's Wager,[59] his philosophical argument, posits that it is better to bet on God than against God.

Pascal used the following logic:

1. God is, or God is not. Reason cannot decide between the two alternatives.
2. A Game is being played ... where heads or tails will turn up.
3. You must wager (it is not optional).
4. Let us weigh the gain and the loss in wagering that God is. Let us estimate these two chances. If you gain, you gain all; if you lose, you lose nothing.
5. Wager, then, without hesitation that He is. (...) There is here an infinity of an infinitely happy

life to gain, a chance of gain against a finite number of chances of loss, and what you stake is finite. And so our proposition is of infinite force, when there is the finite to stake in a game where there are equal risks of gain and of loss, and the infinite to gain.
6. But some cannot believe. They should then "at least learn your inability to believe..." and "Endeavour then to convince" themselves.

Pascal was living in a time when hell was considered far more hellish that we understand it today, if we understand anything. His reasoning was, that it is better to live a good life, have faith in God and get a nice room rather than a damp basement with no view.

People still discuss Pascal's Wager today because, essentially, we are all still in on the wager whether we like it or not—there's no opting out.

~

I leave you with Socrates:

> "To fear death is nothing other than to think oneself wise when one is not. For it is to think one knows what one does not know. No one knows whether death may not even turn out to be one of the greatest blessings of human beings. And yet people fear it as if they knew for certain it is the greatest evil."

REFERENCES

1. https://en.wikipedia.org/wiki/Harry_Patch
2. A revised edition titled *A Lawyer Presents the Evidence for the Afterlife* was published in 2013 by White Crow Books. http://whitecrowbooks.com/books/page/a_lawyer_presents_the_evidence_for_the_afterlife/
3. https://psi-encyclopedia.spr.ac.uk/articles/drop-communicators
4. https://www.arthurfindlaycollege.org
5. https://en.wikipedia.org/wiki/Arthur_Findlay
6. https://thebulletin.org/doomsday-clock/
7. https://en.wikipedia.org/wiki/Astral_plane
8. http://ww.chalicewell.org.uk/index.cfm/glastonbury/About.Home
9. https://www.bahai.org
10. https://en.wikipedia.org/wiki/Silent_Minute
11. "The Wilderness" is an extract from *Private Dowding: The personal story of a soldier killed in battle*, Wellesley Tudor Pole, White Crow Books, Guildford (2012).
12. https://www.psychicnews.org.uk/articles/Lord-Dowding-The-Spiritualist-who-saved-Britain

[13] https://www.britannica.com/topic/theosophy

[14] Frederick Richard Thomas Trench-Gascoigne, (4 July 1851 – 2 June 1937), from the Royal Horse Guards and a DSO in 1900, a well-known soldier and traveler of the day. Source: https://en.wikipedia.org/wiki/Gascoigne_baronets

[15] https://en.wikipedia.org/wiki/Siege_of_Khartoum

[16] I was unable to track down *The Triumph of Life Eternal*. Ed.

[17] "Death on the Battlefield" is a chapter from *Many Mansions*, Lord Dowding, White Crow Books, Guildford (2013).

[18] Automatic writing: writing said to be produced by a spiritual, occult, or subconscious agency rather than by the conscious intention of the writer.

[19] https://www.near-death.com/science/evidence/people-born-blind-can-see-during-nde.html

[20] https://www.youtube.com/watch?v=PL615hI3VjE

[21] http://moonmagazine.org/diane-corcoran-the-near-death-experience-2013-11-02/

[22] https://en.wikipedia.org/wiki/Kerry_Packer

[23] https://iands.org/childrens-near-death-experiences.html#a1

[24] If the reader is looking for data on NDEs a good place to start is www.near-death.com and www.nderf.org

[25] "The Vision of Er," translation: Benjamin Jowett

[26] http://classics.mit.edu/Plato/republic.11.x.html
https://www.biography.com/people/socrates-9488126

[27] *Recollections of an old Soldier: The Life of Captain David Perry* (1741 - 1826)

[28] *If Morning Never Comes: A Soldier's Near-Death Experience on the Battlefield*, Bill Vandenbush, White Crow Books, Hove (2016).

[29] https://www.biblegateway.com/passage/?search=2+Corinthians+12&version=NIV

REFERENCES

30 https://www.biblegateway.com/passage/?search=Acts+9%3A3-9&version=NIV

31 President Roosevelt's secretary communicates from the afterlife" is an extract from *Geraldine Cummins: An Appreciation* by Charles Fryer, White Crow Books, Guildford (2013).

32 "Rescue Circles" is an extract from *The Dark Star*, Lord Dowding, White Crow Books, Hove (2014).

33 http://greaterreality.com/dvmediumship.htm

34 https://en.wikipedia.org/wiki/Spirit_guide

35 *The Psychic Riddle* by Issac K. Funk, first published in 1907 by Funk & Wagnalls company.

36 A Conscious Dissolution is an extract from *The Dead have Never Died*, A. A. Knopf, New York, (1917). It was included in *The French Revelation: Voice to Voice Conversations with Spirits Through the Mediumship of Emily S. French*, ed. N. Riley Heagerty, White Crow Books, Hove (2015).

37 Some information about Hatch can be found here. https://en.wikipedia.org/wiki/Smith_Estate_(Los_Angeles)

38 *Letters from a Living Dead Man: The Anthology*, Elsa Barker, White Crow Books, Hove (2017), contains all 135 letters.

39 https://en.wikipedia.org/wiki/Akashic_records

40 *War Letters from a Living Dead Man*, Elsa Barker White Crow Books, Guildford (2010).

41 https://www.gradesaver.com/goethes-faust/study-guide/summary-walpurgis-night-walpurgis-nights-dream-gloomy-day-field-night-open-field-dungeon

42 *War Letters from a Living Dead Man*, Elsa Barker, White Crow Books, Guildford (2010).

43 https://en.wikipedia.org/wiki/W._T._Stead

44 http://en.wikipedia.org/wiki/John_Jacob_Astor_IV. The Titanic passenger list can be found here. http://en.wikipedia.org/wiki/List_of_Titanic_passengers

45. https://en.wikipedia.org/wiki/John_Jacob_Astor_IV
46. http://magazine.stregis.com/the-house-that-jack-built/
47. http://www.rmslusitania.info/people/lusitania-victims/
48. https://en.wikipedia.org/wiki/Alfred_Gwynne_Vanderbilt_I
49. https://en.wikipedia.org/wiki/Vanderbilt_family
50. http://en.wikipedia.org/wiki/Anna_Held
51. *Letters from a Living Dead Man: The Anthology*, Elsa Barker, White Crow Books, Hove (2017).
52. http://whitecrowbooks.com/michaeltymn/
53. https://psi-encyclopedia.spr.ac.uk/articles/psi-researchers-i#Robert_Hare_1781-1858
54. https://www.biblegateway.com/passage/?search=Luke+15%3A11-32&version=NIV
55. https://www.biblegateway.com/passage/?search=Luke+15%3A4-7&version=NIV
56. https://www.biblegateway.com/passage/?search=John+8%3A1-11&version=NIV
57. https://www.biblegateway.com/passage/?search=Matthew+16%3A19&version=NIV
58. https://biblehub.com/john/14-2.htm
59. https://plato.stanford.edu/entries/pascal-wager/

REFERENCES

White Crow titles quoted in this book include:

If Morning Never Comes: A Soldier's Near-Death Experience on the Battlefield
by Bill Vandenbush
Paperback ISBN: 978-1-78677-002-8
eBook   ISBN: 978-1-78677-003-5

A Lawyer Presents the Evidence for the Afterlife
by Victor Zammit and Wendy Zammit
Paperback ISBN: 978-1-908733-22-1
eBook   ISBN: 978-1-908733-43-6

Private Dowding: The personal story of a soldier killed in battle
by Wellesley Tudor Pole
Paperback ISBN: 978-1-908733-52-8
eBook   ISBN: 978-1-908733-53-5

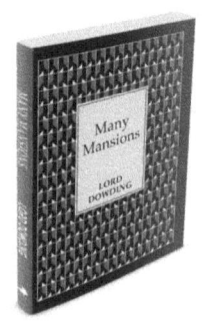

Many Mansions
by Lord Dowding,
Paperback ISBN: 978-1-910121-07-8
eBook   ISBN: 978-1-910121-08-5

Geraldine Cummins: An Appreciation
by Charles Fryer
Paperback ISBN: 978-1-908733-82-5
eBook   ISBN: 978-1-908733-83-2

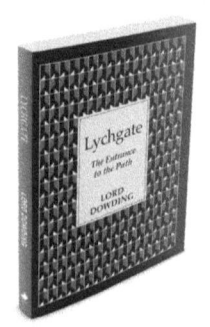

Lychgate: The Entrance to the Path
by Lord Dowding
Paperback ISBN: 978-1-908733-62-7
eBook   ISBN: 978-1-908733-63-4

REFERENCES

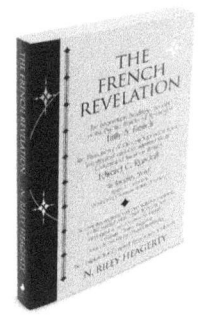

The French Revelation: Voice to Voice Conversations with Spirits Through the Mediumship of Emily S. French
edited by N. Riley Heagerty
Paperback ISBN: 978-1-910121-46-7
eBook ISBN: 978-1-910121-47-4

Letters from a Living Dead Man: The Anthology
by Elsa Barker
Paperback ISBN: 978-1-78677-027-1
eBook ISBN: 978-1-78677-028-8

Thirty Years Among the Dead
by Carl Wickland, M.D.
Paperback ISBN: 978-1-907661-72-3
eBook ISBN: 978-1-907661-73-0